Carol Jones

D0948655

Fully Alive

Fully Alive

Embracing the
Greatest Promise
on the Planet

Rick Baldwin

Printed in Canada

Published in the United States by Baxter Press, Friendswood, Texas. Formatting and cover design by Anne McLaughlin, Blue Lake Design, Dickinson, Texas.

ISBN: 1-888237-60-0
Second Printing

The primary version of the Bible used in this book is the New Living Translation, published by Tyndale Charitable Trust. Used by permission of Tyndale House Publishers.

Other translations include the New International Version (NIV), The Living Bible (TLB), Contemporary English Version (CEV), God's Word Translation (GWT), New Century Version (NCV), and *The Message.*

This book is dedicated to…

My precious wife, Marie. My love for you grows with each passing year. You are indeed "as fine as fine can be."

Our sons, Justin and Daniel. Words can't express how proud I am of you as I see you trusting Jesus and becoming fully alive in Him.

To protect confidentiality, the publisher has changed the names and details in some of the stories in this book.

TABLE OF CONTENTS

ACKNOWLEDGEMENTS

This book is truly the result of a team effort. Among the many who have contributed to make it a reality, I would like to especially thank…

- The people of Friendswood Community Church (FCC) who inspire and encourage me daily, as together we pursue becoming fully alive in Jesus Christ.

- The FCC Board of Directors and Staff who have encouraged and supported this project. Without your talents and passionate contributions, FCC would only be a dream.

- The individuals who labored to transcribe several of my recorded messages into print. My sincere thanks to Carolyn Connelly, Sandra Mooney, Paulette Morgan, and Sue Rives.

- Amy Schendel and Jane Shelby, who have not only encouraged me, but spent countless hours reviewing and editing drafts.

- Pat Springle of Baxter Press, who has been invaluable in crafting and shaping this book. Without Pat's contributions, this book would not have been written.

- My wife, Marie, who not only has been the greatest influence on my spiritual life, but who also spent endless hours editing and shaping the words of this book. Thanks, Marie! You are the best!

- Jesus, who I came to know on a cool October day 21 years ago. In a very real sense, "life" began that day as I began to discover what it means to become fully alive in him.

INTRODUCTION

*O*f all the statements documented throughout human history, the one that holds the most power and promise for our lives was recorded in the Bible in the Gospel of John, chapter 10, verse 10. Jesus Christ stood before a crowd and made this staggering statement: "My purpose is to give life in all of its fullness." The New Testament was written in Greek, a very descriptive language. In this verse the Greek word for fullness, *perissos*, is packed with meaning. Those who heard Jesus that day understood "fullness" to mean "excessively, exceedingly, abundantly above and beyond anything we can imagine." Jesus was saying that the very reason he stepped out of eternity and into time was to shower people—any who would accept it—with so much goodness and grace and vitality of life that it's almost illegal! To experience this much of God's rich love, forgiveness, strength, and purpose is to be *fully alive.* That's what Jesus wanted for those who listened to him that day two thousand years ago, and it's what he wants for you and me today. It is, quite frankly, the greatest promise on the planet.

Though this incredible promise is given to every single person, I would have to say that of the hundreds of people I know, only a handful genuinely and consistently experience being fully alive. That's tragic, because every person longs for that kind of life. For some reason, most of us miss it. How to obtain that life seems to be a puzzle most of us can't solve. Have you ever tried to complete a 1000-piece jigsaw puzzle? It's a daunting task. Many of us look at the

Christian life like we look at a pile of tiny puzzle pieces dumped on the table. The box top shows us what the finished puzzle is supposed to look like, but all we have is a jumbled mass of disconnected pieces that we're supposed to figure out how to put together. We admire the beautiful picture, and we try to find a few pieces that connect, but before long we shrug our shoulders and give up. It's just too confusing…too complex…too hard to sort out.

But here's some very good news. There aren't a thousand pieces to the puzzle. There are only nine—nine facets of the life Jesus wants us to embrace and enjoy. Each one of us can experience these. They aren't contingent on our having lived a perfect life. In fact, Jesus makes this promise to seriously flawed, deeply needy people like me…and probably like you, too. It's not only for people who have the highest IQ's. In fact, we find the simplest people, especially children, enjoyed him most. We don't need a certain social pedigree or religious background to put the pieces together and be fully alive. Jesus' magnificent promise is for *all* people, in *every* age, with *every* conceivable background, with *every* type of need, who are flawed in *every* imaginable way. This promise is universal, but it's also deeply personal. His promise is spoken by his own lips to you and to me.

It is my hope that as you read this book, you will be encouraged in the depths of your soul. There aren't a thousand

Jesus' magnificent promise is for all people, in every age, with every conceivable background, with every type of need, who are flawed in every imaginable way.

puzzle pieces; only a few. They aren't designed to keep us confused; they're meant to give us handles on life. We aren't alone as we try to figure out what it means to be fully alive. Jesus gave us his Spirit and his Word to guide us and shine light on our path. And there are others on the same journey—we can learn a lot from them.

As we look at this magnificent promise, you'll probably realize that you already know some of the principles. They are pieces that have been in your hands all along. Maybe a few insights will be new and fresh to you. Be sure of this: As much as you want to live a life that is fully alive to all the love, joy, peace, and purpose you can possibly experience, God wants it for you even more.

Reading books is of great value to stimulate thinking and teach us principles, but I've found that pointed questions and honest dialogue with friends help me apply those principles more specifically to my own life. Perhaps you will, too. At the end of each chapter, you'll find a section titled "Think about it." Use these questions and exercises to reflect, pray, and consider how God might want to shape your attitudes and actions so you will experience the fulfillment of his incredible promise. These sections are also designed to stimulate discussions in small groups.

THINK ABOUT IT...

1. Is being "fully alive" in Christ a completed puzzle in your mind, or are you still trying to figure out exactly what the pieces are and how they fit together? Explain your answer.

2. What are some reasons you're reading this book? What do you hope to get out of it?

LIFE'S BIGGEST DECISION

*W*e sometimes use the word "faith" to mean no more than intellectual knowledge. A structural engineer looks at his calculations and says, "I have faith that this building can withstand 120 mph winds." But that is not what the word means in the Bible. For the engineer, true faith would be demonstrated by staying in the building as a hurricane with 120 mph winds bears down upon the site.

TRUE FAITH

Intellectual belief acknowledges truth, but it doesn't involve personal commitment. James, author of one of the letters in the New Testament, understood that this kind of belief isn't what God had in mind. James wrote, "Do you still think it's enough just to believe that there is one God? Well, even the demons believe this, and they tremble in terror!" (James 2:19) In the first century, Greek words for "faith," "trust," and "belief" were considered to be synonyms, and writers used these words to communicate that a statement is intellectually true. But the authors of the New Testament found this terminology to be insufficient. Something else was needed to convey more than intellectual assent, so for the first time, they used terms like "trust

To have faith in Jesus meant to radically yield to his leadership and authority.

in Christ," "faith *in* Jesus," and "believe *in* God." To believe in Jesus, they were saying, is not just to know facts about him, but to surrender our hearts, our lives, and our purposes to him. To have faith in Jesus meant to radically yield to his leadership and authority. This kind of *faith* is the first piece of the puzzle. It is the essential cornerstone of living a life that is fully alive.

The most fully alive life I have ever studied is that of a man named Paul, who lived in the first century. It's no coincidence that the distinguishing feature of his life was his radical *faith* in Jesus Christ. Earlier in Paul's life, he had vehemently opposed the Christian faith, trying to eradicate Jesus' followers. Then one fateful day, he met Jesus face to face in a blinding light on a road to the city of Damascus. From that day forward, Paul made a 180-degree turn as he began to radically trust in Jesus. Much of the book of Acts in the New Testament is the drama of his life's purpose lived out in thrilling events in that first century.

Paul would write to the Christians in Galatia, "I myself no longer live, but Christ lives in me" (Galatians 2:20). In effect, he was saying, "I have radically yielded my life to someone else. That someone is Jesus. " He continued, "So I live my life in this earthly body by trusting in the Son of God, who loved me and gave himself for me." That's the statement of a man who had authentic, life-changing *faith* in Jesus Christ. It was a faith essentially defined by placing himself under the absolute leadership and authority of Jesus Christ.

I mentioned that I know a handful of people who are fully alive in Christ. Every single one of those people has radically surrendered himself or herself to the leadership and authority of Jesus Christ. Again, the link between faith and being fully alive in Jesus Christ is no coincidence.

A study by the Barna Research Group shows a startling statistic. Of the Americans who responded to their survey, 80% intellectually acknowledged the Lordship of Jesus Christ, but only 7% showed any signs that they had actually surrendered their lives to him.[1] Those few, though, demonstrated a far higher satisfaction with life, far lower levels of stress, and far fewer life-crippling addictions. The survey concluded that the more deeply committed people are to Jesus, the more likely they are to experience self-confidence, peace, and fulfillment. It makes perfect sense. When we surrender our lives to the One who promises to make us fully alive, that promise is fulfilled, and we experience more joy, love, and purpose than ever before.

Philosophy professor and author Dallas Willard observed that we may be afraid of the cost of following Christ, but we actually pay a much higher price when we don't follow him. Willard calls this choice "nondiscipleship." In his book, *The Spirit of the Disciplines,* he wrote, "Nondiscipleship costs abiding peace, a life penetrated throughout by love, faith that sees everything in the light of God's overriding governance for good, hopefulness that stands firm in the most discouraging of circumstances, power to do what is right and withstand the forces of evil. In short, it costs exactly that abundance of life Jesus said he came to bring.... The correct perspective is to see

---

1   George Barna E-Letter, August 26, 2002.

following Christ not only as the necessity it is, but as the fulfillment of the highest human possibilities and as life on the highest plane."[2]

LOYALTY EARNED

For some of us, when we hear the expression "following Christ" described in terms of "surrender to authority," the hair stands up on the back of our necks. We don't like to even think of the idea of submission and surrender. After all, we're Americans, and our nation was founded on the bedrock of individual liberty! And besides, some of us are born and bred Texans. We pride ourselves in being rugged individualists. No, for many of us the idea of being submissive rubs against the grain.

All of us, however, are under authority in one way or another. Children are under the authority of their parents. Students submit to their teachers and school administrators. Most of us are employed by companies, and we have bosses who exercise leadership over us. Even the most independent people among us are under the authority of the police, state and federal laws, and the IRS. We may not value—and we may even despise—that authority, but we are under it whether we like it or not.

I have learned that not all authority is the same. Under certain leaders we are stifled, while under others we flourish. Under some we chafe; under others we thrive. Under some authority our spirit is gradually extinguished, while under other authority we become fully alive. The critical difference lies in four key areas in the life of the leader:

---

2   Dallas Willard, *The Spirit of the Disciplines: Understanding How God Changes Lives*, (Harper Collins Publishers, San Francisco), 1989, p. 16.

competence, character, power, and compassion. No one has ever come close to matching Jesus' qualifications in these four areas.

The competence of Jesus

For fifteen years I worked for a major oil company. In my first assignment, I worked under the leadership of a man named Bob Keiser. I quickly realized that Bob had a brilliant mind. He understood the oil business exceptionally well. In fact, he eventually became president of the company and chairman of the board. Bob was not only bright; he also had excellent business instincts. In even the most difficult situations, his judgment was sound. For the two years I worked under Bob, I thrived. I loved going to work each day, and I nearly floated home each evening because I thoroughly enjoyed working for someone as competent as Bob.

Two years later, I was transferred to a department to work under a man who had been in the business for 30 years. Even with all his experience, this man had a hard time connecting the dots. In fact, he seemed to lack even the most basic common sense. Instead of looking forward to my work each day, my morale went south in a hurry. After only a few weeks in this new position, my wife, Marie, began to notice a change in my demeanor as I arrived home from work each evening. She asked, "Rick, what has happened at work?"

I replied, "I used to enjoy work so much because Bob was so capable, but now I work for a man who is totally inept! It's as simple as that." I had thrived under competent authority, but I chafed under the leadership of a man who was incompetent. It is painfully frustrating to work for someone who doesn't have the necessary skills to do their job.

Colossians 2:3 says this about Jesus Christ's *competence:* "In him lie hidden all the treasures of wisdom and knowledge." He knows everything, including everything about you. He knows how you are wired and how you respond to people and situations. He knows what it takes for you to thrive, and he knows what kills your heart. King David marveled at God's intimate knowledge of him. He wrote:

"O Lord, you have examined my heart
> and know everything about me.
You know when I sit down or stand up.
> You know my every thought when far away.
You chart the path ahead of me and tell me where to
> stop and rest.
Every moment you know where I am.
You know what I am going to say
> even before I say it, Lord.
You both precede and follow me.
> You place your hand of blessing on my head.
Such knowledge is too wonderful for me,
> too great for me to know!" (Psalm 139:1-6)

> *You and I thrive under Jesus' leadership because he is ultimately and supremely competent.*

Not only does Jesus know everything about you, he knows the past, the present, and the future. There will never be a time when something in your life happens and he grimaces, "I'm so sorry I led you here. I had no idea it would turn out like this." That, I can assure you, will never happen. He is well aware of tomorrow, and he leads you with the sure knowledge of what tomorrow will bring. You and I thrive under Jesus' leadership because he is ultimately and supremely competent.

The character of Jesus

A second trait of Jesus' leadership is his *character*. A few years ago, a man called to make an appointment to see me. He came to my office and told me a troubling story. He worked for a large corporation. In fact, he held a high position in that company. He made a handsome salary, and he was poised to make millions over the next few years. He enjoyed his work and felt good about his contribution to the success of the company, but there was a fly in the ointment. "In the past few months," he said with frustration, "I've realized that the person supervising our division is engaging in some unethical practices. He insists that I participate with him." He paused for a moment, then he continued, "Rick, I cringe under his authority. I've been thinking about this for weeks. I have a lot at stake—my career, the financial stability of my family—but I can't continue to follow this man's leadership. I'm dying there." He looked intently at me, and then he said resolutely, "I've decided to resign Monday morning."

I appreciated his integrity, but I wondered why he was telling me this since he had already made his decision. I asked that question, and he replied, "I just wanted somebody to affirm that I'm doing the right thing." His spirit was slowly being extinguished under the leadership of a man who lacked moral character.

The writer to the Hebrews speaks of Jesus' character as he describes his role as our high priest: "He is the kind of high priest we need because he is holy and blameless, unstained by sin. He has now been set apart from sinners, and he has been given the highest place of honor in heaven" (Hebrews 7:26). Jesus Christ is never unethical, sordid, or tainted by selfishness. And if we follow him, every step we take will be honorable. There will never be a time that we look back and say, "I wish I hadn't followed Jesus because he led me into a moral ditch." That simply won't happen. As we follow the One who is holy, blameless, and pure, there won't be a time that we hang our heads in shame or avert our gaze so people can't look into our eyes. Jesus Christ has a flawless character, and as we follow him, our characters are increasingly aligned with his. We were designed to thrive under this type of authority.

> *And if we follow him, every step we take will be honorable.*

The power of Jesus

The third trait of Jesus' leadership is his *power*. When I was 27 years old, I was given my first major management role in the oil company where I worked. My job was under the authority of Marvin Boyd, a man of great competence and character. Marvin had come to our company through a large acquisition, and in the new organization Marvin was given responsibility without power. We brought him ideas, and he helped shape them into great plans, but he had no authority to put those plans into action. Much of our best work was left on the drawing board never to be acted upon. Marvin's powerlessness discouraged our entire team, as well as Marvin himself.

Five years later, I was transferred to the corporate office in Dallas. I reported to a vice president, but due to the nature of my work, everything I did went directly to the president, Jim McCormick. Once or twice a week, I met with Jim to review proposals and plans. If he liked an idea, he put the wheels in motion to make those plans a reality. He had the power to turn ideas into action, and he exercised that power wisely. The discouragement I felt working with Marvin Boyd (through no fault of his own) was in stark contrast to the excitement I experienced day after day as I worked on plans that I had every hope would be accepted and implemented by Jim. I thrived under his authority.

Just before Jesus ascended back to heaven, he met with his followers on a hillside in Palestine. He told them, "I have been given complete authority in heaven and on earth" (Matthew 28:18). Not *some,* not *a lot,* but *all* of the mighty power of the universe is under his control. It doesn't get any bigger than that! John tells us that Jesus Christ made everything that has been created—from the most minute atom to the galaxies with hundreds of billions of stars. Yet remarkably, the pinnacle of his creation is you and me!

In addition to creation power, Jesus also has transformation power. We see this power on display as we watch individuals turn from selfishness to joyfully serving God and others. We also see this power demonstrated when bitterness is washed away by forgiveness as marriages and families are restored by God's love. And Jesus also has resurrection power. He conquered death itself by stepping out of the tomb, and he promises that those who believe in him will conquer death, too. We thrive under his leadership because he has incredible power to accomplish his will in and through us.

The compassion of Jesus

Jesus' unparalleled competence, pure character, and awesome power are directed by the fourth trait of his leadership, his *compassion*. In my career in the oil business, I once worked for a man who was one of the most skilled and competent oil executives I had ever known. His ethical standards were high, and he had ample authority to carry out his plans. But this man didn't give a rip about those of us who worked for him. To him we were expendable assets to use and discard when we no longer served his purposes. As the months went by under his leadership, I felt exploited. All he cared about was the bottom line, the numbers at the end of each quarter. Everything and everyone were valuable only if we met *his* goals. Even if his drive for personal success burned up everyone in his path, he simply didn't care. Working for him was the worst experience of my career. This man had the first three characteristics in spades, but he lacked compassion, and that made all the difference.

Later I worked for a man named Jim Amyx. Jim was a gifted leader who genuinely cared about people. As I spent time with him, I was quickly convinced that in every decision, large or small, Jim would carefully consider the impact upon those of us who worked for him. His actions reflected that he valued us as people. Jim's compassion motivated us to bring our best efforts to the table every day. Our team thrived under Jim's leadership.

We never have to question how much he cares because his message of love was literally nailed down for us when he died on the cross.

In the same way, we thrive under the leadership of Jesus because he cares so deeply for us. We never have to question how much he cares because his message of love was literally nailed down for us when he died on the cross. The night he was betrayed, he told his followers, "And here is how to measure it—the greatest love is shown when people lay down their lives for their friends" (John 15:13). His words had even more power less than 24 hours later as he hung suspended from the cross, dying so that his friends might live. The measure of his love is that he paid the ultimate price for you and me.

The One who has all power and authority is also the One who loves tenderly and deeply. At a dark time in the history of the children of Israel, they accused God of deserting them. But through the prophet Isaiah, God said, "Can a woman forget her nursing child? Will she have no compassion on the child from her womb? Although mothers may forget, I will not forget you. I have engraved you on the palms of my hands" (Isaiah 49:15-16 GWT).

More than anyone who ever lived, Jesus embodies all four of these leadership characteristics. He is completely *competent,* has perfect *character,* and holds *all power* in his hands. All of these traits are fueled by the deepest, broadest, highest *compassion* ever known. Under his leadership, we thrive because we feel both loved and challenged to partner with him to accomplish his purpose to change lives.

Jesus isn't looking for only strong, brilliant, mature people to make them fully alive. He's looking for anyone who is willing to say "yes" to him. Nothing eliminates us; not our flawed family background, ethnicity, social standing, or secret sins. To become fully alive, we only have to say "yes" when we hear his voice.

Are you wondering how a person's life might change if Jesus had complete leadership over it? Let me tell you the story of someone I know.

SHE WOULD HAVE MISSED ALL THIS!

Throughout most of her life, Mindy Robertson had virtually no relationship with her father. She was, in essence, a fatherless child. Her parents had married when they were very young, and soon her father began a life of substance abuse. His pain and anger escalated, and he began abusing Mindy's mother. The couple soon separated, then divorced. For a few years, Mindy's father occasionally stepped in and out of her life, but when she was 13, he walked away and didn't look back.

When Mindy was 22, a man broke into her apartment and beat her beyond recognition. For days she lay in the hospital. Her family, including her father, came to see her, but his message was far from comforting. He told her that because he had come to see her, he had lost his job. He blamed his abandoned, beaten, broken daughter for his troubles! That was enough. Mindy determined then and there that she would walk through the rest of her life without her father.

A few years ago, Mindy and her husband Ramsey began attending our church. One day as we talked, I asked Mindy when her spiritual life began. She told me that she had rarely gone to church before she started attending here. Then she said something that warms the heart of any pastor. She told me, "Rick, I'll never forget what I heard the first time I came to this church."

I waited with anticipation to hear her talk about the profound impact of my teaching and the pearls of wisdom

I had shared on that Sunday morning. I, of course, would then humbly say, "Oh, it wasn't me. It was the Lord." Expectantly, I asked her, "What was it that I said that changed your life?"

"It wasn't what you said," she related. (I was deflated now!) "When the offering plate was passed, the Associate Pastor, John Wise, announced that visitors were not expected to give any money, but to accept the service as a gift. That meant a lot to me, so we kept coming. Not long after that, I began to trust in Jesus."

In the weeks, months, and years that followed, Mindy found that Jesus Christ is not like anyone she had ever known. In fact, he is quite the opposite of her earthly father. Mindy found Jesus' love and compassion for her to be deep and unwavering. She found his guidance to be filled with wisdom. She found his power to influence her life and circumstances to be nothing short of supernatural.

> *Mindy found that Jesus Christ is not like anyone she had ever known.*

As wonderful as these insights were to Mindy, that's not the end of the story. She continued to grow as a follower of Jesus, and she listened with her heart as she read in the Bible that God wants to mend broken relationships. Mindy learned that God wants us to forgive those who have hurt us, and he wants us to honor our father and mother. Because she was trusting Jesus to lead her, she knew she needed to act on what she was learning. She realized she needed to love her father for who he was, instead of resenting him for not being the father she wanted him to be. She took the bold step of sending her father a Christmas card and calling him on the phone. To her surprise, she found that Jesus had been at work in his life during the 12 long years since they had last seen each other. They had a wonderful conversation, and both wanted to see one another again.

Their plans to get together were sidetracked by a number of things that happen in active families, including her daughter's broken arm. Yet Mindy's dream of being reunited with her father was as strong as ever. Months later, she got a phone call from a young girl who introduced herself as Mindy's half-sister. She told Mindy that her father had come to town hoping to see her, and she asked if Mindy would be willing to meet with him. Mindy was thrilled! She immediately said, "Yes!"

Mindy's father and half-sister came to her home, and they had a wonderful time together. They had so much to catch up on, and they shared the missing pieces of their lives. Mindy's father took lots of pictures of her and his granddaughter. He told her with obvious excitement, "I can't wait to show these pictures to all my friends and the people at work!" Before they left, her father looked her in the eyes and told her, "I want you to know that I love you, and I'm so proud of what you've made of your life."

Only days later, the phone rang, and the caller told Mindy that her father had been in a terrible car wreck. She and Ramsey immediately drove to Louisiana to be at his side. In her father's room in intensive care, Mindy told him how much she loved him. He couldn't speak, but he asked for a piece of paper. He carefully wrote, "Tell God I'm sorry." More loving, affirming notes passed between father and daughter, and in those few days, God brought incredible healing to both of them. Years of anger and pain melted away in the warmth of love and forgiveness. But soon, Mindy's father lost his fight to live.

Mindy's emotions understandably ranged from elation at being reconciled with her father to sorrow over losing him. She had just gotten her father back…then he was gone. In this heart-wrenching moment, Mindy could have shaken her fist in anger at God. But she didn't. She chose again to put herself under his loving leadership, trusting that he knows and cares more deeply than she could possibly imagine. After the funeral, she wrote me, "I've been given many wonderful gifts from God in my lifetime, but the gift of that one, last visit with my father was nothing short of a miracle. I will treasure that time with him for the rest of my life. I know now more than ever that God will take care of me, and that his love is so powerful. He gave me back the one thing that was lacking in my life. He gave me back my father."

The next Christmas, Mindy and Ramsey wanted to give one last gift to her father. They bought a headstone for his grave, and on it they had inscribed Jesus' promise to one of the men hanging on a cross next to him. It reads, "I assure you, this day you will be in Paradise with me."

Think of what Mindy would have missed if she had not put herself under the leadership of Jesus Christ and had not taken that gut-wrenching, risky step of reaching out to mend the broken relationship with her father. If she had not listened to Jesus and followed him, she would have missed one of the biggest thrills of her life: having her relationship with her father restored. And if she hadn't held onto God's greatness and goodness when her father lay dying in the hospital, bitterness might have caused her to miss the wonder of giving and receiving love from her father before he died. But because she was fully alive to

Jesus' love and leadership, Mindy experienced more joy than she ever thought possible.

HOW ABOUT YOU?

Are you fully alive in Christ? Are you one of the 7% who experience the reality of Jesus' competence, character, power, and compassion, or are you still on the outside looking in? If we aren't trusting in Jesus, we're trusting in a substitute—a poor substitute—to give us fulfillment and direction. But God has made us so that only he can fill the hole in our hearts. Nothing else fits. The truth is that nothing else even comes close. The biggest questions in your life and mine are these: Who do we trust as our ultimate authority? To whom do we entrust our hearts, our desires, our dreams, and our futures? Who are we following?

Most of us trust in our own ability to make life work. Yet as I grow older, I'm increasingly aware that my wisdom is so often lacking, my character is still flawed, my strength fails, and my compassion sometimes runs dry. But if I put myself under the authority of Jesus Christ, all of his resources become available to me. I tap into *his* competence, my character is shaped and conformed to *his*, I trust in *his* power, and as I experience *his* compassion for me, *his* love and compassion flow through me to others.

The first piece of the fully alive puzzle is faith that Jesus Christ is worthy of being our leader because of his competence, character, power, and compassion. This faith is far more than just intellectual acknowledgement that he lived, taught, and died at a point in history. This faith is the transfer of our loyalty from anything or anyone else to Christ. We become his—body and soul—and we desire to please him in everything we do. It's Christ who makes us fully alive.

I've talked to hundreds of men and women, young and old, who desire to live fully alive in Jesus Christ. It begins by expressing a definitive "yes" to his gracious invitation to follow him. Have you said "yes" to Jesus? You may have been on the outside looking in, but now you want to jump in with both feet and submit to the loving leadership of the God of the universe. You can express your "yes" to him in words that are your own, or you might pray something like this:

Jesus, you have proven your power by creating the universe, and you've demonstrated your love by dying for me on the cross. You are a loving, powerful leader, and I submit myself to you. I want to be loyal to you, to let you work deeply in my heart, and to allow you to use me in any way you choose. Thank you so much for forgiving me and making me a new person. Thank you for beginning the work of making me fully alive!

The moment you and I put our trust in Christ, some significant things happen to us. Let me list just a few of them:

- We have a change of eternal address (John 5:24).

- All of our sins are completely forgiven (Ephesians 1:7).

- We are adopted by God into his family, and we are his dearly loved children (Romans 8:15).

- The Holy Spirit takes up residence in us (1 Corinthians 6:19-20).

- Jesus himself begins to live in us (Galatians 2:20).

Nothing—absolutely nothing—is more wonderful than to be forgiven, loved, and accepted by God. Perhaps you have said "yes" to Christ sometime in the past, and you have had at least a taste of being fully alive, but for some reason, that relationship has become stale. Has your heart been moved by Jesus' invitation to come to him and by his promise to make you more fully alive? If it has, tell him so. He'll be thrilled to hear it.

THINK ABOUT IT...

1. In your life, who is the person (in your family, at work, at church, or anywhere else) who is most trustworthy? What are some characteristics of that person that give you confidence in his or her competence, character, power, and compassion?

2. Which of the four characteristics of Jesus described in this chapter is most meaningful or attractive to you? Explain your answer.

3. Based upon what you have read in this chapter, describe what the Bible means when it speaks of having "faith in Jesus."

4. Read Isaiah 49:15-16. What are some things that might cause us to think that God has deserted us? Describe the tone and content of God's response in this passage to those who think he has deserted them.

5. Is there anyone, yourself included, who could do a better job of leading your life than Jesus could? Explain your answer.

6. Have you come to the point where you are consistently yielding *everything* in your life to the leadership and authority of Jesus? If not, what are you excluding from his leadership? Is there any reason you would not want to trust him with this as well?

7. Would you say you are certain you have a relationship with Jesus Christ, you think you do but aren't sure, or you're still thinking about it? If you aren't sure, what is the next step in your journey to find and follow Jesus?

CHAPTER

2

OXYGEN FOR THE SOUL

O ne Saturday a few years ago, I got a call from my friend Phil Harris. He told me that his mother, who had been in vibrant health for 81 years, had been diagnosed with cancer. The urgency of the call, though, wasn't because of the diagnosis. Phil explained that his mother had to be rushed to the hospital because she was having difficulty breathing. With each labored breath, she was gasping for air. A few days later I saw Phil and asked him about his mother. He told me, "She's still in ICU, but she's feeling really good." I guess I looked surprised because he then explained, "The doctor put her on oxygen, and that's made all the difference."

The second piece of the puzzle for living a life fully alive in Jesus Christ is *prayer*. It is the oxygen for our souls. Connecting with God in meaningful ways is absolutely essential to spiritual health. We may be able to endure a short while without it, but soon we weaken and gasp for the life-giving air we receive when we communicate with the One who made us and loves us.

> *Connecting with God in meaningful ways is absolutely essential to spiritual health.*

Phil's mother was on the edge of life and death because she couldn't breathe, but when she received oxygen, she revived—and in fact, she thrived. What oxygen did for her physically, prayer can do for us spiritually.

Jesus said that the reason he came to earth was to give life in all its fullness to every person. He listed no financial, social, religious, or intellectual qualifications. He gave no age restrictions or blackout dates when we can't experience life to the fullest. Paraphrasing John 10:10, Jesus said, "I'm making a blanket, universal promise to anyone who will accept my offer. Every person who takes me up on my offer will become fully alive. No exceptions. Are you in?" If we aren't experiencing the kind of life Jesus promised, maybe there are some pieces of the puzzle that are missing. The first one, faith, is a corner piece. When I try to work jigsaw puzzles, I look for a corner to get me started. That single piece often helps me make sense of everything else. Faith in Jesus Christ as our leader, our authority, and our Lord is the corner piece in our puzzle. Once faith is in place, prayer is the next vitally important piece. When we locate it and find where it fits in our lives, we then tap into the heart of God and the vast resources he has made available to us.

WITH EVERY SUNRISE AND THROUGHOUT EACH DAY

We can become more fully alive by praying with every sunrise and throughout each day. The people I know who are fully alive in Christ may stagger to the coffee pot the first thing in the morning, but it isn't long until their minds clear and their hearts breathe in the life-giving oxygen of truth and grace through prayer. This habit may have begun with simple discipline to carve out some time each morning, but soon the motivation changes from discipline to thirst. Ironically, the more we are satisfied by drinking in the life of Christ, the thirstier we are for his love, wisdom, and power. King David developed this passion of beginning the day with prayer. He wrote, "Listen to my voice in the morning, Lord. Each morning I bring my requests to you and wait expectantly" (Psalm 5:3).

> *Ironically, the more we are satisfied by drinking in the life of Christ, the thirstier we are for his love, wisdom, and power.*

Did you get that? He waited "expectantly." He wasn't just going through the motions of a dry, mechanical habit. He was connecting with the God of the universe, the One who is the author of life and holds "all the treasures of wisdom and knowledge." For David, prayer wasn't empty conversation. He expected God to speak to his heart, guide his steps, and work in his circumstances. He reflected on God's truth, God's will, and God's ways, and he asked for wisdom about how to respond to the opportunities and challenges that faced him that day. Then he waited. He expected God to give him the direction and the strength he desperately needed in order to do what pleased the One who loved him so much.

David wasn't the only person in the Bible who felt the need to make prayer the first priority in the morning. Jesus, God in the flesh, the One who created all things, felt the need to connect with God the Father before the day's events got too hectic. Mark wrote in his gospel, "The next morning Jesus awoke long before daybreak and went out alone into the wilderness to pray" (Mark 1:35). If the Son of God needed to pray with every sunrise, how much more do you and I need to spend time with God at the beginning of each day?

People who are fully alive in Christ also realize the need to connect with God at many points throughout the day. Paul encouraged his readers, including you and me, to "pray continually" (1 Thessalonians 5:17 NIV). That means to pray as a spontaneous reflex to the myriad of events in our day. As we drive our children to school, we can pray for their friendships and their choices. When we talk to a troubled friend on the phone, we can silently ask God for wisdom to say the right thing. In business meetings and at ballgames, in traffic jams and doing housework, with our oldest friends and our newest acquaintances, morning, noon, and night, we can talk with God, inviting him into the details of our lives. Praying throughout the day also begins with determined discipline, but it soon becomes an unconscious habit of "bringing God into the now" of every moment of our lives.

GOD IS WAITING...

For some of us, the concept of communicating with God is brand new. We've never done it before. Some of us, though, enjoy a rich, meaningful, interactive relationship with God, and prayer is essential in that relationship. But for others, prayer may have become a stale ritual, empty of meaning. Regardless of your experience with prayer, the stunning fact is that God is

He waits to talk with you, to guide you, and to act on your behalf.

waiting patiently for you to connect with him. He waits to *talk* with you, to *guide* you, and to *act* on your behalf.

To talk with us

After all these years, I still find it astonishing that *God is waiting to talk with us*. After all, he is the One who created the entire universe. He is the One who is known as the "Holy One of Israel." While that is true, he is also the One who uniquely, personally crafted you down to the DNA imprinted upon your every cell. In Isaiah 43:1, God says, "Do not be afraid, for I have ransomed you. I have called you by name; you are mine." The author of Hebrews tells us that all who have faith in Jesus (the first piece of the puzzle) are given direct access to God. We are encouraged, "So let us come boldly to the throne of our gracious God. There we will receive his mercy, and we will find grace to help us when we need it" (Hebrews 4:16).

The truth is, God is waiting to talk with us. Sometimes I need visible reminders of that fact. A few years ago I spoke about the thick curtain that hung for centuries in the temple in Jerusalem separating the people from the area known as the "Holy of Holies." This curtain symbolized the separation between people and God that is caused by sin. History records that two thousand years ago, at the precise moment when Jesus died on a cross just outside Jerusalem, the curtain in the temple was ripped from top to bottom without being touched by human hands! (See Luke 23:44-46.) At that moment, access to the presence of God was opened to every person who would place their faith in Jesus—to the priests who stood in amazement looking at the torn curtain, to the crowd watching the limp body of Jesus as it was taken down from the cross, and to you and me today. All barriers have been removed, and God waits for us to communicate with him.

At the end of the message that Sunday, we gave out small pieces of cloth to each person in attendance. We suggested that if they wanted to accept Jesus' offer of forgiveness and receive access to God the Father, that they tear the cloth. The sound of ripping filled the auditorium that day. A week or so later, I received an anonymous gift of a piece of torn cloth placed in a beautiful frame. That priceless gift hangs on my office wall. Sometimes when I pray, I look at that torn cloth as a reminder that the price has been paid and God has granted me access to the throne of grace. He is waiting to talk with me and with you.

I have another reminder in my office. (It seems that I need several reminders that the God of grace is waiting for me!) Someone gave me a small lighthouse with a light bulb in the top. I turn it on when I go to the office, even if it's on a weekend when I'm just checking email. Like a lighthouse waiting and watching for passing ships, God is waiting and watching for me. I need these reminders because the truth that Almighty God is waiting for me is almost too wonderful to believe. Many times as I've started to pray, I've said to God, "Lord, even though I'm busy and distracted, and even though the miracle of being in your presence is hard to comprehend, I know you're waiting to talk to me."

Do you need a reminder? I encourage you to find a symbol of God waiting to talk to you. The symbol may be elaborate or simple, a spoken phrase or a tangible object. Whatever it is, let it remind you often that the Creator who spoke and flung the galaxies into space focuses his attention on you. He is infinite, so he can focus his mind and heart on each of us at the same time.

To guide us

The second truth about prayer is that *God is waiting to guide us.* We often talk and sing about *our desire* to follow Jesus, but there's a bigger truth: He desires, he longs, and he waits expectantly for us to follow him. When we grasp his loving desire, our own longing is inflamed and purified. In a confusing world of conflicting passions, we have a desperate need to understand God's guidance and find his path. Not long ago, I told a story about unethical conduct in corporate America. I've seldom spoken on this issue, even in a passing manner. After that message, a man stopped me in the hall. He looked worried, and he told me that he, too, was under pressure from his company to engage in unethical behaviors. He said, "For the past couple of weeks, my daily prayer has been, 'God, I need your help! I need you to guide me so I'll know what to do at work.' And today, as I drove up to the parking lot at church, I prayed that same prayer again." With a tear rolling down his cheek, he told me, "Today, as I listened to the story you told, I knew God had answered my prayer. Can we talk for a minute?"

He told me more about his situation, and we shared some thoughts about how the goodness, wisdom, and sovereignty of God provide steppingstones for the path God wanted him to travel. He walked away that day with a fresh sense of direction, and on Monday morning went to his boss's office. In that meeting, he told his superiors that he didn't feel at all comfortable with some of the things he'd been asked to do for the company because those actions were wrong. But he didn't stop there. He told his boss how he had prayed for guidance, had heard a message at church, and had talked to his pastor. He explained that he now knew what he needed to do. He told his boss, "I'm not the only one concerned about our business practices. Someone much bigger than me is concerned about what's going on in this company, and he wants things to be done ethically." Some of his colleagues heard about his conversation with the boss, and they were both amazed and encouraged by his boldness to speak the truth.

When I lack God's guidance and rely on my own limited knowledge and wisdom, I'm prone to error, sometimes with serious consequences. In my better moments, I know I'm foolish to act on partial, and sometimes incorrect, information when the One who has all knowledge is waiting to guide me.

When I was young, we lived on the grounds of the old Fort Ringgold in deep South Texas, an area rich in military history. It was a great place for a boy to grow up. We lived in the midst of old army barracks, military parade grounds, and the stories of battles won and lost virtually in our backyard. One of these battles, the Battle of Palmetto Ranch, was fought May 13-14, 1865, a few miles down the Rio Grande River. The Texans fought for the Confederacy. In this battle, the Southerners were outnumbered and out-gunned, but with skill and courage, they gradually turned the tide of the battle. By the end of the second day, they had lost many men from their ranks, but they had won the field. It was a glorious victory for that little army, but soon, elation turned to heartache. Communication was slow in those days. No cell phones or email. No planes or cars. Not even regular mail service. Those men fought and died at Palmetto Ranch without knowing that their commander, Robert E. Lee, had surrendered at Appomattox Court House more than a month before. Without clear communication with their leader, these men invested all they had—their courage, their skills, their blood, and their futures—for nothing!

As I look at my own experience, I see times when I've done the same thing. I thought I knew exactly what I should do. I invested all my abilities, all my knowledge, and all my energy, but the result was a disaster because I had not taken time to get directions from my leader, Jesus Christ. Good intentions aren't enough. We are *designed* by God to be *directed* by God. Then and only then are all of our God-given abilities channeled to accomplish his purposes his way. James tells us that God's guidance is there for the asking. He wrote, "If you need wisdom—if you want to know what God wants you to do—ask him, and he will gladly tell you. He will not resent your asking" (James 1:5). That doesn't mean God dispenses his wisdom like answers from a child's Magic 8-Ball. It's not

> *We are designed by God to be directed by God.*

magic, and it's not always immediate. Sometimes God wants to teach us to pursue him, so he delays giving us wisdom until we truly long for him to work any way he chooses. When we experience delays or confusion, it doesn't mean God doesn't want to give us guidance. It only means that he has additional things (like patience and perseverance) for us to learn in addition to wisdom.

When life is confusing and difficult, it's natural for us to think that God has forgotten us or that he really doesn't know what he's doing. These thoughts may not be clearly articulated in our minds, but we may come to the conclusion that we know more than God about how to run our lives. Our knowledge, though, is limited and flawed. God's insight about every person and every circumstance, however, is infinite and perfect. In the last 50 years, man's knowledge has grown enormously in medicine, science, and technology. Yet all the knowledge we have gained so far, and all we will ever gain on this earth, is only a droplet on a single wave in the vast ocean of God's infinite knowledge. As we increasingly realize that he truly knows all things, we trust him more and more to guide our lives.

To act on our behalf

Another truth that gives life and vitality to our prayers and injects oxygen into our souls is the fact that *God is waiting to act on our behalf.* He is patient, but he certainly isn't passive. He waits for us, and at times, he wants us to wait for him. But whether he is quick or slow, when the time is right, he acts decisively and powerfully. Even a casual reading of the Bible leads us to the clear conclusion that when God is ready, he moves! Of course, God often graciously acts in us and through us even when we don't ask him, but there are times when he won't act until and unless we ask. James wrote, "And yet the reason you don't have what you want is that you don't ask God for it" (James 4:2). In many cases, it's that simple.

Over the years, God has given me many wonderful friends. A few years ago, a man with exceptional musical talent and I became good friends. He and I share two passionate interests: sports and spirituality. We're both sports fanatics, but his allegiance and mine are for different schools. (That doesn't seem to be a problem for him when his team thoroughly trounces mine!) We enjoy talking about our schools and our teams, and we also enjoy talking about spiritual things. Early in our relationship, my friend told me that he wasn't sure what to make of the claims of Jesus Christ. In our many times together, he asked questions, and I answered them as best I could. We talked about how an infinite God could become a finite human being, how someone could be raised from the dead, how the Bible, though written long ago, was still relevant today, and a host of other topics.

We often met at a fast food restaurant to talk about sports and God, usually in that order. One day I realized that I had told him everything I've ever known or thought about God. I'd been praying for him before, but now I realized that *all* I could do was pray. It was up to God to work in his heart. I keep a journal of my prayers, and if you looked at my journal during that time, you'd find my friend's name written down day after day. I prayed that God would reveal himself to my friend in a powerful, unmistakable way.

One gray, cloudy morning, the two of us sat in the restaurant. After a while, our conversation drifted to spiritual things again. After some discussion, I thought it was time to be completely open and honest with him. I looked him in the eye and said, "What is holding you back from giving your full allegiance to Jesus Christ?"

He nodded knowingly, hesitated, and then told me, "I love my music, but I'm afraid that if I give my life to Christ, he'll take that talent away from me. I just don't think I can handle that. I don't want to lose an important part of who I am."

Instantly, I smiled and told him, "Don't you realize that God is the one who gave you that talent? He's not going to take it away."

At that exact moment, the clouds parted and a shaft of bright sunlight pierced the gloom of the sky and illuminated the booth where we sat! From what I could tell, it was the only sunlight coming through the dark clouds. The sudden brightness took his breath away. Both of us sat in stunned silence for a few seconds. We were awestruck. Then I just laughed and said, "This is no coincidence. It means that if you give your life to Christ, you'll experience the joy of your talent more than ever before. This sunlight on our booth right now is the hand of God showing himself to you." It was an electrifying moment!

God might have made that sunlight pierce the dark clouds and shine on that one booth at that particular moment even if I hadn't prayed, but I doubt it. I think he was waiting for me to ask him to work powerfully in my friend's life. A few short months later while sitting in that same restaurant my friend said, "I did something this week that might be of interest to you. I placed my faith in Jesus Christ." Might be of interest to me? He knew it would be the best news he could ever give me!

Day after day, God is waiting for us to say to him, "Lord, I have something that's really important to me, but I can't pull it off on my own. If you'd act, I'd really appreciate it. I don't know the best way or the best time, but you're God. I'm not. I trust you to work in this situation. Thank you." When we pray like that, I think God is thrilled because he delights in his children coming to him with our needs and trusting him to be the Almighty, loving Lord in the details of our lives.

Just remember that God waits to *talk* with you, he waits to *guide* you, and he waits to *act* powerfully and specifically in your relationships and circumstances. If you need a symbol to remind you of these encouraging truths, find it, use it, and let it bring you back again and again to these bedrock facts about the heart of God.

A PATTERN FOR PRAYER

Sometimes I realize that my prayers have become nothing more than asking God for help. There's nothing wrong with asking, but I have learned my conversations with him are richer and more meaningful when they are more balanced. Quite often I use the acronym, P-R-A-Y, Praise... Repent...Ask...Yield, to keep me from getting stuck in the "Help!" mode. If you find yourself doing the same thing, the following pattern of prayer may be beneficial to you.

> *My conversations with him are richer and more meaningful when they are more balanced.*

Praise

First, I focus on *praising* God for two things: I praise him for who he is, and I praise him for what he has done. I look at passages of Scripture that help me see him more clearly. I tell God about qualities I appreciate in him. I marvel at his infinite knowledge and wisdom, I celebrate his limitless power, and I thank him for loving me, especially the love he displayed from the cross. The psalms are prayer journals of David and a few others who wrote out their prayers. These prayers are full of honest emotion, just like my journals, and many of the psalms express heartfelt praise and thanks to God. Psalm 145 is one of my favorites. I turn there often to refresh my mind and heart·

about the character of God. Read slowly and thoughtfully these words David wrote.

"The Lord is kind and merciful,
    slow to get angry, full of unfailing love.
The Lord is good to everyone.
    He showers compassion on all his creation.
All of your works will thank you, Lord,
    and your faithful followers will bless you.
For your kingdom is an everlasting kingdom.
    You rule generation after generation.
 The Lord is faithful in all he says;
    he is gracious in all he does.
The Lord helps the fallen
    and lifts up those bent beneath their loads.
All eyes look to you for help;
    you give them their food as they need it.
When you open your hand,
    you satisfy the hunger and thirst of every living thing" (Psalm 145:8-10, 13-16).

Then I thank God for what he has done. I am as specific and personal as I can possibly be. An example of David praying this way is recorded in the following psalm:

"I will praise you, Lord, for you have rescued me.
    You refused to let my enemies triumph over me.
O Lord my God, I cried out to you for help,
    and you restored my health.
You brought me up from the grave, O Lord.
    You kept me from falling into the pit of death"
(Psalm 30:1-3).

Repent

The second aspect of prayer is to *repent,* to clear away anything that has come between God and me. In our home, when there's tension between Marie and me or the boys and me, our communication is not what it should be. At those times, we're more interested in protecting ourselves from hurt than in loving, giving, and sharing. When that happens, each of us needs to take the initiative to say those incredibly powerful words, "I was wrong. I'm sorry for what I've done. Please forgive me." That clears the air and restores the channels of communication. It's the same way in our relationship with God. Often when I pray, I make it a regular part of my prayer to ask, "Lord, is there anything between us that needs to be resolved? Have I done or said anything harmful toward you or others?" And then I sit and listen. Sometimes the answer is, "Yes, Rick. Do you remember…?"

At that moment, I can be defensive and say, "Yeah, but he deserved it!" or "Well, you just don't understand, God. I just couldn't help it." But on my better days, I respond, "Yes, Lord, you're right. What I did was wrong. I'm sorry."

God has given us a fantastic promise to count on when we repent. In John's first letter, he wrote, "But if we confess our sins to him, he is faithful and just to forgive us and to cleanse us from every wrong" (1 John 1:9). The slate is wiped clean, because the price for our sin was already paid two thousand years ago on a hill outside Jerusalem.

Confession means "to agree with." When I confess and repent, I'm agreeing with God that my actions, words, or attitudes were wrong, but I also agree with him that my sin has been forgiven. I acknowledge to him that I don't intend to repeat that sin because it dishonors him and devalues those I've hurt. Because I realize how costly my forgiveness is to God, I'm genuinely thankful for his grace and mercy to wipe my sins away.

We know King David as one of the great kings of Israel and a passionate man who sincerely loved God. But David also committed some of the most awful sins recorded in the Bible. He committed adultery, then tried to cover it up by having the woman's husband murdered. He hoped no one would notice, but God did. When he was confronted with his sin, he recorded one of the most moving psalms in the Bible. As you read his confession, imagine his heartache because of his sin and his relief as he experienced God's forgiveness.

"Have mercy on me, O God,
    because of your unfailing love.
Because of your great compassion,
    blot out the stain of my sins.
Wash me clean from my guilt.
    Purify me from my sin.
For I recognize my shameful deeds—
    they haunt me day and night.
But you desire honesty from the heart,
    so you can teach me to be wise in my inmost being.
Purify me from my sins, and I will be clean;
    wash me, and I will be whiter than snow.
Oh, give me back my joy again;
    you have broken me—now let me rejoice.
Create in me a clean heart, O God.
    Renew a right spirit within me.
Restore to me again the joy of your salvation,
    and make me willing to obey you"
(Psalm 51:1-3, 6-8, 10, 12).

Do David's words also express your heart? One of the greatest gifts from God is that he forgives our selfishness, deceit, rage, petty jealousy, pride, cruelty, apathy, and other sins of every kind. As we recognize the seriousness of our sins and the wonder of God's forgiveness, we'll be amazed at his grace, and we'll want to please him more and more.

Ask

The third part of this model of prayer is *asking* God for absolutely anything. Nothing is too big or too small. In my relationship with my boys, they can come to me with any need and every opportunity. If it matters to them, it matters to me. That's God's attitude as he relates to us, too. Sometimes, God chooses to act right away to answer our prayer, but sometimes he delays for any number of reasons. And sometimes he knows what we requested isn't the best thing, so he says, "No." I've talked to men and women who realized later that if they would have received what they requested from God, their lives would have been radically—and negatively—changed. They were so grateful that the Lord said "No" to them. God's answers are always designed to build our faith. He gives us quick and marvelous answers so we know he is both mighty and present in our lives, and he makes us wait while he purifies our motives or arranges circumstances so that the best result is accomplished. Whether he answers immediately and magnificently, causes us to wait, or says "No," we can trust that his infinite wisdom and infinite love guide his hands. And we can rest in that.

Yield

The fourth component of this model of prayer is to *yield* to Jesus' leadership and authority. In the first chapter, we talked at length about Jesus' unsurpassed qualifications to be the leader of our lives. We reflected on his complete *competence*, his perfect *character*, his limitless *power*, and his infinite *compassion*. I find it invaluable each and every morning to clearly yield once again to Jesus' authority—to yield my thoughts...my emotions...my words...and my actions to his leading.

> *I find it invaluable each and every morning to clearly yield once again to Jesus' authority.*

In the pages of the Bible, we find many compelling incentives to yield our lives to the leadership of Jesus Christ, but I want to focus on one particular reason. Paul tells us that the desire to honor the One who loves us so much serves as a powerful motivation. He wrote, "Whatever we do, it is because Christ's love controls us. Since we believe that Christ died for everyone, we also believe that we have all died to the old life we used to live. He died for everyone so that those who receive his new life will no longer live to please themselves. Instead, they will live to please Christ, who died and was raised for them" (2 Corinthians 5:14-15).

And listen

After praising, repenting, asking, and yielding in your time of prayer, take some time to be silent and listen to God's Spirit. Prayer isn't meant to be a one-way affair. Dallas Willard, author of *Hearing God*, wrote, "People are meant to live in an ongoing conversation with God, speaking and being spoken to."[3] As you listen, God may remind you of a passage of Scripture that addresses a concern you've prayed about, or he may give you an insight to help you make a decision. He may direct you to talk to a wise, trusted friend about a concern, or he may nudge you to take some specific action. God "speaks" to us in many ways, most often through his word, the Bible, and the still, small voice of his Spirit. He also "speaks" through wise friends, the beauty of nature, worship music, and many other sources of truth and hope. His message to us is always in line with the truth of Scripture, so be sure to check any impressions with the clear teaching of God's word.

THE FIRST STEP

All of us want to be fully alive, and a key piece of the puzzle is to have a vibrant life of prayer. It's oxygen for our souls. We desperately need to be connected to our loving leader, the One who knows all about us. The first step is to carve out some time with each sunrise to spend with God...time when we aren't multi-tasking...time just with God, with no competing distractions. Find a quiet place where you can be alone to read, think, and pray.

The first step is to carve out some time with each sunrise to spend with God... time when we aren't multi-tasking... time just with God, with no competing distractions.

---

3   Dallas Willard, *Hearing God*, (InterVarsity Press, Downer's Grove, IL, 1984), p. 18.

If this is new to you, I recommend that you make a commitment to God to spend 10 minutes with him at the beginning of each day. I made this commitment 21 years ago when a growing family and a demanding corporate job occupied every waking minute. I was a new follower of Jesus and believed spending time with him was essential for my life. It sounds silly now, but I carved out the 10 minutes with two minor changes in my lifestyle. I began to shave at night rather than in the morning, and I quit glancing at the sports page before going to work. (This was a major sacrifice for a self-acknowledged sports junkie!) As the years unfolded, I found this time with God to be so rich that the original 10 minutes has grown much longer.

If it's not possible to spend this time with God at the beginning of your day, find the time in your schedule that works for you. Consider using your lunch hour, when your children are napping, or at the end of the day.

As you spend this time with God, I recommend that you incorporate reading a brief passage from the Bible (more on this in chapter 3). I find it helpful to keep a notebook and pen close by to jot down my thoughts and prayers. Consider using the model of prayer described in this chapter, and remember that you are spending time with the God who created every particle in the vast expanse of the universe and who knows every hair on your head. He is incredibly mighty, and he is incredibly kind. That's the one you are reading about and talking with—and that realization will change your life. Remember, he is waiting....

THINK ABOUT IT...

1. In what way is prayer "oxygen for the soul" for people who desire to be fully alive in Christ?

2. Look again at Mark 1:35. If Jesus needed to spend time alone with the Father early in the morning, what does that say about our need for prayer first thing each day? Is that your practice? If it is, what does this time mean in your life? If not, what are your plans to begin this practice?

3. One of the most important points in this chapter is that God longs to meet with us even more than we want to meet with him. What person do you long to interact with in rich, meaningful ways? How does that desire help you understand and appreciate God's desire to interact with you?

4. Review the section about God waiting to talk with us, guide us, and act on our behalf. Which of these concepts is most meaningful to you? Explain your answer.

5. Read Psalm 51. What do you think David was thinking and feeling as he wrote this psalm? How does it communicate the seriousness of sin without leaving us wallowing in oppressive guilt?

6. Take a few minutes to experience the model for prayer outlined in this chapter.

- *Praise*—Focus on a characteristic of God mentioned in this book, and praise God for that quality. Think about things God has done to provide you with material possessions, work, health, family, friends, and other things you value, and thank him for these gifts.

- *Repent*—Ask God to reveal anything in your attitude, words, or actions that displeases him. Tell him you are sorry and thank him for his forgiveness.

- *Ask*—Read and think about James 4:2. What are some things you want to ask God for right now?

- *Yield*—Reflect on how you can trust Jesus' leadership and tell him that you yield yourself to him today.

- And finally, take some time to *listen*.

CHAPTER 3

A ROADMAP FOR THE JOURNEY

*J*ust after my sophomore year in college, I took a job for the summer with an oil company working offshore south of Louisiana. Early one morning, I said "goodbye" to my parents, and I took off for my summer adventure on an oil production platform. The drive to the site was about 600 miles from my home in South Texas. I had carefully charted the best route on a map. The directions I had plotted took me on back roads through the swamps of Louisiana. About 50 miles from my destination, I passed through a little town. The last rays of sunset had vanished, and it was pitch black outside. I was feeling good. Actually, I was really excited about my new job and the adventure awaiting me.

About four miles past the little town, I was driving along at 60 miles an hour. Suddenly my headlights revealed a barricade in the road! I slammed on my brakes and skidded to a stop just short of a line of barrels blocking the road! After a long sigh of relief, I got out of the car to see what was going on. I was astonished. The headlights of my car showed that there was no road past the barricade! The pavement just ended! I quickly reached into the car and unfolded my map. Yes, I was on the correct road. I had no idea where to go from there, so I drove back to the small town and pulled into the gas station.

I took my map to the man behind the counter and unfolded it. I told him, "Sir, I'm trying to get to Intercoastal City, Louisiana. My map says to take that road right there." I pointed to the road that was barricaded.

He leaned over and looked at the map. Then with a smirk of disgust, he tossed my map aside and said, "Son, your map is wrong. Let me tell you how to get to Intercoastal City." He reached under the counter and pulled out a different map. He showed me the roads I needed to take. I thanked him for the directions, and I started to reach for my map. Then I thought, *Why should I take that map with me? It was wrong once. It will more than likely be wrong again.* I left that map behind and drove off to Intercoastal City—this time with the correct directions.

If you and I have the wrong roadmap for a trip, we might take some wrong turns and waste our time. The problems we encounter almost surely will make us late in arriving, and unforeseen difficulties might even be hazardous to our health. This analogy applies to our journey through life, too. If we choose the wrong roadmap for life's journey, we waste precious time while we try to figure out where we are and where we should go. We might not ever reach our goal, and our very lives might be in danger. In this chapter, we'll look at a fully trustworthy roadmap: the Bible.

Let me put our need for a roadmap in the context of the greatest promise on the planet. Jesus Christ gave us the most powerful promise ever uttered. He said, "I have come for the purpose of giving you life in all of its fullness. In fact, my sole reason for coming to earth is to make you an offer to become fully alive" (John 10:10). We have compared our search for this life to putting the pieces of a puzzle together. The first piece is *faith* in Jesus Christ, not just intellectual assent to facts about Jesus, but entrusting our hearts, our desires, and our futures to the loving leadership of Jesus Christ. This kind of faith changes lives. The second piece of the puzzle, *prayer,* is meaningful interaction with the God of the universe at every sunrise and throughout the day. If faith and prayer become deeply established in our lives, we will have a great start in becoming fully alive in Christ.

The third piece of the puzzle is a rich, deep grasp of *God's word.* When we talk about reading and studying the Bible, some of us think, *Oh, I tried that, but it didn't work. Have you ever really tried to read the Bible? It must be for retired or very religious people.* I'd like to dispel that misconception. The Bible is for all of us: the bright and the simple, theological professors and the newest Christ-followers, young and old. God wants all of us to know how to use his word as a roadmap to guide us through life. In the pages of the Bible, we find the deepest truths about God's greatness and goodness, we see how we

> *The Bible is for all of us: the bright and the simple, theological professors and the newest Christ-followers, young and old.*

can have the richest relationships, and we find that our lives can count for more than we ever imagined. That's what God's roadmap will do for us! If the Christian life is new to you, you're in for a real adventure. If you're an old hand at Bible study, maybe some things in this chapter will warm your heart. Let me start with some principles that are important to all of us.

THE BIBLE IS GOD'S WORD

The Bible stakes the claim that it is God's unique communication to us. It stands apart from all other writings. As Paul writes in 2 Timothy 3:16, "All Scripture is inspired by God." Peter writes in 2 Peter 1:20-21 (TLB), "For no prophecy recorded in Scripture was ever thought up by the prophet himself. It was the Holy Spirit within these godly men who gave them true messages from God." In these verses, the term "no prophecy" means "no words," which tells us that everything that was written is directly given by God.

Years ago when I was searching for spiritual truth, I explored whether the Bible could back up this claim of being God's unique communication to us. In brief summary, this is what I found. The Bible has proven to be *a remarkably accurate historical document.* During most of the 19th and the first half of the 20th centuries many scholars considered the Bible to be a poor history book because many of the people, events, and civilizations mentioned could not be verified through any other source. However, in the last fifty years archaeology has confirmed biblical accounts in more than 25,000 sites![4] To this date, archaeology has yet to refute a single biblical claim! This is unprecedented among writings and is all the more remarkable considering the Bible is actually a collection

In the last fifty years archaeology has confirmed biblical accounts in more than 25,000 sites!

---

4   Paul E. Little, *Know Why You Believe,* (Intervarsity Press, Downer's Grove, Illinois), 1988, revised 1999.

of 66 books written by over 40 authors from 3 continents spanning a period of over 1200 years.

Biblical prophecies have repeatedly proven accurate. For example, Psalm 22:16-18 (TLB) states, "The enemy, this gang of evil men, circles me like a pack of dogs; they have pierced my hands and feet. I can count every bone in my body. See these men of evil gloat and stare; they divide my clothes among themselves by a toss of the dice." Clearly this is a description of crucifixion. Remarkably, this was written 600 years before the Persians, in the 4th century B.C., first "invented" this grizzly form of execution. In addition, the practice of throwing dice for the criminal's clothing was first practiced in the 1st century, B.C. by the Romans. Hundreds of other similar biblical prophecies have come true.

As a spiritual seeker, this evidence helped me come to a point of believing the biblical claim that the Bible *is* God's unique communication to us. If you would like to delve further into this area, I recommend the following books: *The Case for Christ* by Lee Strobel; *A Search for the Spiritual* by James White; *Know Why You Believe* by Paul Little; and *A Ready Defense* by Josh McDowell.

A PERSONAL LETTER WRITTEN TO US

The Bible is not a general communiqué from God to mankind. As only he could do, God made it a "living letter" that can speak directly into our lives and our present circumstances, whatever they might be. These two passages make this point:

- "For the word of God is full of living power. It is sharper than the sharpest knife, cutting deep into our innermost thoughts and desires. It exposes us for what we really are" (Hebrews 4:12).

- "All Scripture is inspired by God and is useful to teach us what is true and to make us realize what is wrong in our lives. It straightens us out and teaches us to do what is right" (2 Timothy 3:16).

I am in awe of how God can take words written so long ago and speak specifically to what I am dealing with today. Fourteen years ago, I was wrestling with a major life decision. I knew God was leading me to quit my career in the oil business, go to seminary, and become a pastor. I had numerous excellent arguing points about why this wasn't a good idea. Early one morning during my usual time with God praying and reading the Bible, I told God there were two obvious reasons why I knew he didn't really want me to become a pastor: I assumed we would never own a home again, which seemed decidedly un-American, and we would be leaving my aging parents in Texas when we moved to Kentucky to attend seminary. That didn't seem like a good way to "honor my parents." After concluding my prayer, I opened the Bible to Luke 9 where I had ended the day before. I was stopped "dead in my tracks" by these words:

"As they were walking along someone said to Jesus, 'I will follow you no matter where you go.' But Jesus replied, 'Foxes have dens to live in, and birds have nests, but I, the Son of Man, have no home of my own, not even a place to lay my head.' He said to another person, 'Come, be my disciple.' The man agreed, but he said, 'Lord, first let me return home and bury my father.' Jesus replied, 'Let those who are spiritually dead care for their own dead. Your duty is to go and preach the coming of the Kingdom of God' " (Luke 9:57-60).

By the time I finished reading, I realized that my arguments with God were toast! How amazing that he would provide such a timely answer to my two biggest concerns in four short verses! In my experience over the last 21 years, I have consistently found God to use Scripture to speak clearly and personally into my life. That is just what the passages in Hebrews 4 and 2 Timothy 3 promise it will do.

FULLY TRUSTWORTHY

Finally, we can *fully trust God's word.* The authority and veracity of the Creator and Sustainer of the universe stands behind every statement in the Bible, so we can trust everything in it: history and philosophy, ethics and practical living, the character of God and the needs of people. As we read, we don't have to ask, "Is this really the truth?" or "If I follow God's leading, will it mess up my life?" Everything in the pages of God's word is accurate. Proverbs 30:5 assures us, "Every word of God proves true."

THE TRANSFORMING POWER OF THE BIBLE
It transforms how we think.

God uses the Bible to transform the way we *think* about God, about ourselves, about our purpose, and about others. I often see things through my own limited and skewed perspective. Isaiah quotes God as saying, " 'My thoughts are completely different from yours,' says the Lord. 'And my ways are far beyond anything you could imagine. For just as the heavens are higher than the earth, so are my ways higher than your ways and my thoughts than your thoughts' " (Isaiah 55:8-9). God strategically uses the Bible to help us see things as he sees them. He offers us wisdom and insight. Psalm 19:7-8 states, "The decrees of the

Lord are trustworthy, making wise the simple…. The commands of the Lord are clear, giving insight to life." God's word is our benchmark to know what's true. Then we can measure our thoughts against his standard and change our thoughts to fit the truth.

For example, let me tell you about a man I met several years ago. I'll call him Tom. As I watched him and got to know him, my respect for him grew. One day, he came to talk with me, and he said, "Rick, let me pull the curtain back and tell you what's really going on in my life." I nodded, and he continued, "Back in my younger years, I made some bad mistakes. To be candid, I committed some really bad sins. It's been many years now, and I've become a follower of Christ. But when I go home and visit my parents, they bring up the mistakes I made. They throw them back in my face over and over again." Tom looked dejected, then he told me, "It's not only them; it's my wife, too. At some point every week—and sometimes many times a week—she brings up those old mistakes. Her conclusion—and her accusation—is that I'm worthless, good for nothing, and I've ruined her life, the kids' lives, and my life. Rick, I feel pretty hopeless right now." He sighed, "I wonder if I ought to continue living."

I wanted to challenge the basic assumptions of the messages Tom had received. I told him, "With that kind of input from your parents and your wife, I can understand why you feel so dejected. But Tom, if God has a different opinion of you and of your worth, value, and purpose—an opinion that is the opposite of the opinions your wife and your parents have of you—who would be right?"

He thought for a few seconds, then he said, "Well, if God really has a different view of me, then I would have to say that my wife is wrong…and even my parents are wrong." The lights seemed to go on in his heart, and I saw a glimmer of hope in his eyes.

I handed him a Bible, and I told him, "Tom, I want you to begin to read this book. Let me write down some passages that will be particularly helpful for you." I listed some scriptures that explain God's forgiveness and our new identity as loved, forgiven, and accepted children of God. Then I looked him in the eyes and said, "If you'll fill your mind with God's truth about who you are, it will change your life. I promise."

Tom and I met together to talk from time to time. At one point, I gave him an assignment to read and think through Psalm 139, which speaks clearly of God knowing everything, being everywhere, and creating everything in the universe, including each one of us. He came back to see me about a week later. With eyes full of hope, Tom related, "Rick, for the first time in my life, I'm completely convinced that my birth wasn't just an accident. This psalm tells me that God uniquely crafted me—me! He intentionally made me exactly like I've been made!"

As we talked, Tom was still troubled about the terrible sins he had committed. His countenance dropped, and he told me sadly, "But I ruined my life. I guess I can't be who God wants me to be after all."

I asked him to read and reflect on Psalm 51 before we met again. About a week later, Tom came to my office, and again, his eyes were full of hope. Tom had read David's confession of sin and God's gracious forgiveness. I explained to him that David had committed adultery and murder. Tom looked at me with tears in his eyes and asked, "And God forgave him *for that?*"

I nodded, then Tom smiled, "Then he can forgive me, too."

He got it. God used his word to transform Tom's thinking and perception. Now, he looked in the New Testament and read the familiar story of the cross with new eyes. He realized that the price Christ paid to forgive sins wasn't just for everybody else. It was for him, too! That day, I watched the power of God's word convince this man that he was truly forgiven. For the first time in his life, Tom believed that in God's eyes, his sins were past history—forgiven and forgotten.

A few weeks later, Tom and I met to talk about the fact that God has a purpose for every person who is still breathing—not just the people who appear to have perfect lives, not just the ones that haven't made big mistakes, but for every person that's still drawing breath. God has a purpose for all of us. And that day, I watched as Tom began to believe that God indeed still has a purpose for him, too. The transformation from despair to hope in Tom's life didn't happen overnight, but it happened. As we talked for those weeks and months, I could tell that God was changing Tom's thinking.

After a year of reading and reflecting on God's truth about himself, Tom realized that his life had great value to God. The transforming power of truth convinced him that he was fully forgiven because of Christ, and he recognized that God has a unique, meaningful, challenging reason for him to live. By the power of God's word, Tom's mind and heart, his direction in life, and his relationships were eventually transformed.

When we open the pages of the Bible, the first question to ask is: "*What does God want me to know* in this passage I'm reading?" God's truth reaches down into the secret places in our hearts to reveal our deepest motives, and it carries us to new heights of understanding God's incredible power and grace. As we read, we can learn the truth about ourselves. Some of us hear bitter accusations and lies from those around us. And some of us are in relationships with people who think

> *When we open the pages of the Bible, the first question to ask is: "What does God want me to know in this passage I'm reading?"*

God is about as relevant today as a buggy whip. We can simply absorb all the messages we hear each day and let them push us down the wrong road, off the roadmap God wants us to follow. Or we can hold all these messages up to the light of God's truth to see which ones are right and which are wrong. In the light of his truth, our identity, our motivations, our purposes, and our desires become clear. We find how to have the best family relationships, friendships, and dating relationships. We discover the meaning and purpose of money and sex. In the pages of God's word, we uncover wisdom about the hottest topics facing us today: abortion, homosexuality, the environment, wealth and caring for the poor and elderly. It's all there, and it's the one trustworthy roadmap to reshape our minds. No, it's not indexed and listed with convenient questions and answers. We have to dig a little, but our efforts will result in a wealth of gold!

It transforms how we feel.

Another purpose of the Bible is to *transform how we feel*. The truth of God's word is not only for our heads;

it also speaks to our hearts. David wrote, "I have hidden your word in my heart" (Psalm 119:11). I missed this insight for a long time. For many years, I thought the Bible was useful only to change my thinking patterns. I had never thought of letting God's truth transform my emotions. The "heart" is the seat of reflection, and it includes both thoughts and feelings. In essence, David was saying, "God, I have taken

I had never thought of letting God's truth transform my emotions.

your word all the way to the depths of my heart, to the center of my emotions." In the psalm David wrote to show that God's truth transforms our minds, he reminds us that it transforms our emotions, too. He wrote, "The law of the Lord is perfect, reviving the soul.... The commandments of the Lord are right, bringing joy to the heart" (Psalm 19:7-8).

As I watched Tom respond to God's word over the year we met together, I saw his soul revived and his heart filled with joy. When Tom first pulled back the curtain and told me about the anguish in his heart, the word that best described his emotions was despair—utter despair. As the months unfolded and he listened to the truth, his emotions changed from hopelessness to hopefulness. Of course, Tom didn't have just one emotion. He experienced the full range of feelings. He felt anticipation that God would speak to him again and again through the Scriptures. He felt tremendous relief because he became convinced that the sins that had long oppressed him were fully forgiven. He felt a strong, deep sense of peace in the truth and love of God, and he was genuinely excited as he learned that

God's magnificent purpose for him was still waiting to be fulfilled. Tom experienced new freedom and joy. To be honest, his parents and his wife didn't change during this time. They continued to berate him with snide comments and bitter slanders, but Tom became a person of joy because he was taking the word of God into his mind *and* heart.

The transformation of our hearts by God's word doesn't mean, however, that our feelings will always be happy, pleasant, and serene. To be fully alive in Christ means that we care about the same things God cares about. We rejoice when love and justice prevail, but we feel genuine anger and sorrow when we see people experience cruelty and injustice. As we become more fully alive, we will have honest emotions, just like Jesus and the psalmists did. David described a full range of emotions in a single psalm, Psalm 119:

- Joy: "I will never forget your commandments, for you have used them to restore my joy and health" (verse 93).
- Anger: "I am overwhelmed with rage, for my enemies have disregarded your words" (verse 139).
- Comfort: "Your promise revives me; it comforts me in all my troubles" (verse 50).
- Hope: "You are my refuge and my shield; your word is my only source of hope" (verse 114).
- Sorrow: "Rivers of tears gush from my eyes because people disobey your law" (verse 136).
- Freedom: "I will walk in freedom, for I have devoted myself to your commandments" (verse 45).

As I've visited with people over the years, I'd have to say that many of them don't feel comfortable with their emotions. Some have experienced a great deal of pain, and they don't want to experience any more of it. They put a clamp on their emotions, but that clamp doesn't distinguish between positive feelings and painful ones. *All of them* are tightly clamped down. Others believe that "good Christians" should never feel anger or sorrow, so they simply won't allow themselves to feel those emotions. But I'm convinced that a person who is fully alive in Christ experiences the full spectrum of feelings. Certainly, some of the expressions of anger (such as rage) are sinful and wrong, and some expressions of sorrow (such as depression) debilitate the soul. But we don't need to throw away the healthy expressions of our hearts because the extremes are unhealthy. We need wisdom to know which feelings are healthy and which are destructive, and we need to look at the model of Jesus who, as the perfect man, experienced and expressed deep and authentic emotions. For example, Paul tells us—in fact, he commands us—to be angry (at things like offenses and injustice), but to be careful not to sin when we're angry (Ephesians 4:26). The *feeling* of anger, then, isn't wrong. It's a natural and normal response when others hurt us. But we need to be careful not to be involved in angry *actions* to take revenge on those who have offended us. That's the balance God wants for us.

So what does God want us to feel? For me, a good spiritual check is to read a passage in the Bible, and ask the question, "Based upon what I have just read, *how does God want me to feel?*" If I've been reading about the crucifixion and my heart doesn't break with sorrow, something is wrong with either my perception or my heart. If I read about the resurrection and my heart doesn't soar with anticipation and hope, then I know something's hindering my grasp of God's truth. If I read about the exodus when God parted the sea and gave freedom to his people and I'm not thrilled that I, too, have been set free by God, then God's message isn't sinking deeply enough into my soul. When I think about people in our community who live broken lives, in broken families, with broken hearts, if my own heart is not broken for them, then my heart has become hardened and needs to be softened by the grace of God. How does God want us to feel? He wants us to be fully alive, fully connected, emotionally engaged people who respond not only with our heads but also with our hearts. And it's God's word that is our trustworthy roadmap to reshape our emotions.

It transforms the way we act.

The third purpose of the Bible is to *transform the way we act.* James tells us that the word of God changes our behavior as much as it changes our thinking and emotions. He wrote, "...humbly accept the message God has planted in your hearts, for it is strong enough to save your souls. And remember, it is a message to obey, not just to listen to. If you don't obey, you are only fooling yourself" (James 1:21-22). As I read a passage, I ask the question, *"What does God want me to do?"* The Scriptures address life's most difficult issues as well as its most common ones. Here are a few:

- Suppose your best friend has betrayed your trust. How does God want you to respond to that friend?

- Suppose you've come home from a busy day at work and your spouse is cranky and snarls at you. What response would please God?

- Suppose a friend calls you and tells you in an excited voice, "I've heard the most interesting news about Sarah! Let me tell you about it." How does God want you to respond to your friend who is eager to spread gossip?

- Suppose you are on a business trip, and one night you get back to the hotel bone tired. You pick up the remote control, scroll through the pay-per-view listing, and find some movies that you'd never want your spouse or kids to know you watched. What does God want you to do at that moment?

- Suppose you go to your favorite fast-food restaurant for lunch, and as you stand in line, you notice a homeless man standing behind you. He asks, "Excuse me. Do you have money for something to eat?" How does God want you to respond to this man?

- Suppose your boyfriend or girlfriend says, "Let's move in together." What does God want you to do with that request?

Think of my friend, Tom. He was becoming fully alive, and yet his wife often reminded him of his past sins and expressed her unvarnished disappointment that she had ever married him. How did God want Tom to respond to her? As he gained insight from the Bible, he believed God was directing him to take a couple of steps. First, he read in Ephesians that he should "love his wife like Christ loved the church." Since God loves us even when we're at our worst, Tom determined to love the socks off of her, no matter how she treated him. He also decided to pray for her. When he told me his plan, I thought it was great. To be honest, I didn't expect any change except in Tom's heart. I lost touch with Tom for a while, but about two years later, he came to see me and said, "Rick, let me tell you what's happened. I don't know how to explain it other than it is God's doing, but for the first time, my wife has fully forgiven me! The past is no longer an issue in our relationship. We're beyond that now. We've grown so much closer than I ever imagined possible, and our home is completely different. I look forward to coming home at the end of the work day now!" God transformed Tom's actions, and he worked through Tom's courage and compassion to also transform his wife's heart.

As we read the Bible, God transforms our *thinking*, our *emotions*, and our *actions*. As we look at the life of Jesus, we learn to act as he would if he were in our shoes. Spiritual transformation isn't magical, but it is spiritual. We read and study God's word, and God's Spirit works powerfully to change us from the inside out. It's available for all of us. If people can read, a whole world of truth is waiting to be discovered. If people can't read, there are CDs or tapes, or they can find someone to read to them. Even small children—and maybe *especially* small children—can be transformed by God's word. David wrote, "As your word unfolds it gives light and even the simple understand" (Psalm 119:130 New Jerusalem Bible). Are you brilliant? God's word will challenge you to think more deeply than ever before. Are you simple? God's word clearly teaches you wonderful truths about God's kindness and encourages your heart.

I know what you're thinking. You've been reading this chapter and you think, *Yeah, Rick's all excited about the Bible, but he's been to seminary. And good grief, he gets paid to read it! I don't know…it's a mighty big book, and I don't even know where to begin. Besides, who has the time anyway?* If that's what you're thinking, don't despair. Yes, it's a big book, but all of us can gather gems if we'll only take the first steps and begin the search.

A FEW SUGGESTIONS

Let me give you some practical suggestions to help you study God's word.

Develop a vision of how God will use his word in your life.

First, consider the benefits of what you'll learn and how God will use his word to transform your life. Listen as others talk about what they've learned. Ask questions about their motivation, their successes and struggles, and the tangible results of reading and studying. Ask yourself, *How will my life—my relationship with God, my relationships with my family and friends, my sense of peace, the direction of my life, my choices about money and time, my progress in becoming fully alive in Jesus Christ—be better as I gain insight and courage from God's word?* Developing a vision for the impact of your efforts will fuel your motivation!

Use a modern translation.

Find a modern translation that is easy for you to read and understand. Most of us struggle to understand the traditional King James Version because the English language has changed so much in the last 350 years. There are numerous excellent, accurate modern translations to choose from today, including the New Living Translation, the New International Version, and The New Revised Standard Version. Many people find it helpful to get a Bible that includes "Life Application Notes." You can find most versions with these notes included. You may find it helpful to go to a Christian bookstore and read some passages in several different translations. Choose the one you find most readable.

Start in the New Testament.

You will find the Bible much easier to follow and understand if you first read the New Testament, then go back and read the Old. Gradually read through the entire Bible. Go slowly. Pace yourself so that God's truth can transform you at the deepest level.

> *Pace yourself so that God's truth can transform you at the deepest level.*

Use your morning prayer time to read a short passage of Scripture.

I find God often speaks to me through his word about the very things I am currently praying about.

Ask three penetrating questions.

Based upon the passage you have read:
- What does God want you to know?
- What does God want you to feel?
- What does God want you to do?

Be consistent, stay consistent.

And finally, like many things that are good for us, we need to make a habit of soaking our minds in the truth of God's word. In fact, do it nearly every day. Like exercising our muscles, regular study in the Scriptures makes us strong. If we miss a day or two, we keep going on the strength we've developed. But if we miss too many days, our faith muscles begin to atrophy. Doubt and confusion begin to take the place of truth and faith.

BECOMING FULLY ALIVE

God has created us with hearts that long to be fully alive, with all pistons firing and all flames burning brightly. But only God can make us fully alive. He made us with a desperate need to be connected to him in a vital, life-transforming way. He speaks to us through his word, which is our roadmap to give us hope, direction, and purpose. It may be an ancient book, but it's more relevant than today's newspaper because it deals with things that don't change through the centuries: the character of God and the human heart. I'm convinced we can't be fully alive if we aren't acquiring wisdom and encouragement from God's word. Begin where you are. Make a firm decision to carve out time each day for the next month. Begin in the New Testament with a notebook and pen in hand. As you read, answer those three questions, and expect God to reveal himself to you. He will.

THINK ABOUT IT...

1. What is the "roadmap" you have been using to give guidance to your life? (Today's hottest talk show host, a trusted friend, your own reason and intuition?) Has your roadmap proven fully trustworthy? Explain your answer.

2. Read 2 Timothy 3:16-17 and Hebrews 4:12. How does it affect our expectations if we truly believe that the Bible sitting on our shelf is actually "God's word" to us?

3. For an example of how the Bible can transform how you think, feel, and act, read Psalm 1:1-3. Based upon these verses:

   —What does God want you to *know?*

   —What does God want you to *feel?*

   —What does God want you to *do?*

4. This chapter tells us that being fully alive means we experience a full range of emotions. What are some emotions Jesus experienced? (For examples see Matthew 9:36, Matthew 26:37, Mark 3:5, Luke 10:21, Luke 19:41.) Are there any you are hesitant to let yourself feel? Explain your answer. What would it mean for you to be fully alive in Christ in your emotions?

5. What are your plans for beginning or continuing to read and study God's word? According to what you've read in this chapter, how will you know when and if your life is being changed by your study of the Scriptures?

4

A HEART UNLEASHED

*T*wo days ago Marie and I attended the largest worship service of our lives. Over 75,000 people joined us in spite of the near 100-degree heat. Many arrived an hour early in excited anticipation. Entire families came—grandparents, parents, and children. Most had marked this one day on their calendars as much as a year in advance to assure their being there. At least half had driven over a hundred miles for the historic event, filling every hotel within a 50-mile radius. Everyone was dressed to honor the object of our worship—it was truly a beautiful sight. Some waved small banners of praise. Many stood the entire four hours of the televised event. Every few minutes, the crowd erupted in thunderous applause. The sound of tens of thousands singing praises filled the stadium air. There were no strangers. All of us were there for one purpose only—to honor the Fightin' Texas Aggie football team as they went into battle!

Eerie, isn't it, that the description of a football game can sound more like a worship event than the description of many of our church services? To be honest, there are times that more true worship occurs at a sporting event than occurs on a Sunday morning at church. You see, worship is the heartfelt expression of reverence, adoration,

> *Worship is the heartfelt expression of reverence, adoration, and devotion to someone or something.*

and devotion to someone or something. It can be worship of anything—even a football team that doesn't win as often as I desperately would like them to!

WIRED TO WORSHIP

Psychologists as well as theologians tell us that everyone is wired to worship. We all have the need to worship someone or something. Maybe you've observed a junior high girl who worships the boy sitting across from her in math class. She doesn't know his last name, and she has never spoken to him, but she "worships the ground he walks on." Reverence, adoration, and devotion accurately describe her heart toward him. I saw an old friend not long ago who introduced me to his new bride. From the way he spoke about her, the way he hung on her, and the way he was treating her, I could tell he worshiped her.

I worked with a man back in my business days who worshiped the stock market. Although he had a great income with our company, he worked a second job just so he could invest more in the market. He called his broker several times a day, and his emotions rode up and down with the market. Until I became a follower of Jesus 21 years ago, I worshiped corporate success. I would have never admitted it to anyone, but inside I knew my heartfelt passion for corporate advancement was nothing short of worship.

STILL EMPTY

We can worship anyone or anything. The catch is that we will only be satisfied if that someone or something is perfect. When that person or object is the expression of perfection, we sense it is worthy of our worship. My friend who introduced me to his new bride—I lost track, but this was bride number four or five—worshiped his previous brides just as much. He longed for a wife to fill the God-shaped hole in his life, but none of them could. They may have been wonderful women, but they couldn't possibly fill the vacuum God created and designed for himself alone. With each new wife, my friend discovered flaws and imperfections, and his heart would sink like a lead balloon. His worship would fade, with the marriage soon to follow.

I experienced the same emptiness with corporate success. Five and a half years into my career, I received a major promotion that I was certain would bring the contentment I had been pursuing. After a flush of excitement that lasted all of two weeks, the same gnawing emptiness returned. I began to question whether corporate success was worthy of my "worship." Jeremiah had the answer to my question, as he wrote, "The wisest of people who worship idols are stupid and foolish…Say this to those who worship other gods: 'Your so-called gods, who did not make the heavens and earth, will vanish from the earth' " (Jeremiah 10: 8,11).

THE ONE WHO UNLEASHES OUR HEARTS

I have since learned that *anything* that falls short of perfection will eventually disappoint us and leave us disillusioned. When I grasp this, I can understand why the

Bible says, "You must worship no other gods, but only the Lord, for he is a God who is passionate about his relationship with you" (Exodus 34:14). Only God, who is fully competent, has perfect character, possesses all power, and has infinite compassion, can prove worthy of our heartfelt reverence, adoration, and devotion. Only in worshiping him are our hearts unleashed. Only then do our hearts soar. Only then do we become more fully alive.

THE FOURTH PIECE OF THE PUZZLE

The beginning of our journey toward becoming fully alive is *faith* in Jesus Christ—a faith that leads us to follow him. This is the first piece of the puzzle. The second piece is *prayer,* which represents honest, authentic conversation with God. The third piece of the puzzle is *Bible study* where God teaches us, speaks to us, and guides us. The fourth piece of the puzzle is *worship,* in which we express our heartfelt reverence, adoration, and devotion to God. I often take the first letters of reverence, adoration, and devotion, RAD, to remind myself that God is worthy of my radical worship of him.

A FRESH IMAGE OF WORSHIP

> *To worship God "in spirit" means to worship him at a soul level, from the depths of our being.*

So how do we worship God? What does it look like when we worship him? Jesus identified two essentials in worshiping God. He said, "True worshipers will worship the Father in *spirit* and in *truth*. The Father is looking for anyone who will worship him that way" (John 4:23).

To worship God "in spirit" means to worship him at a soul level, from the depths of our being. It means to express reverence, adoration, and devotion to him with genuine heartfelt passion. To worship God in spirit would not be to stand in church and sing through the words of a praise song while you think about lunch plans. To worship him in spirit would be to think deeply and honestly about the words as you sing them directly to God, telling him how you feel about him. When I think about worshiping from a soul level, I can't help but think of the football game we attended two days ago. There were people present who were expressing their devotion to the team from the depths of their being. Their actions left no doubt that they worship Texas A&M football with a passion. That same level of authentic, heartfelt passion is what Jesus had in mind when he spoke of worshiping God in spirit.

When Jesus talked about worshiping God "in truth," he was teaching us the importance of worshiping God for who he really is, not who we might imagine him to be. We all form ideas of what God is like based on our family backgrounds and experiences. Some of the preconceptions may be accurate, but some may be terribly wrong. One of the key benefits of Bible study is that we discover God's true nature. With consistent study of the Bible, those who think God to be harsh and cruel will find that he is gentle, humble, and kind. Those who think of him as absent or distant find that he is closer than our breath. Those who believe God has no interest in their lives find that his loving thoughts are always upon them. Those who think he is unconcerned with our behavior find that he is a loving father who disciplines his children.

> *Many of us are at risk of seeing God's love and grace, but failing to see his holiness, his justice, and his power.*

Many of us today, myself included, are at risk of seeing God's love and grace, but failing to see his holiness, his justice, and his power. Author and psychologist Larry Crabb observes that many of us think of God as "a specially attentive waiter."[5] When we get good service from him, we give him a nice tip of thanks or praise. When we don't get what we want, we gripe about the poor service. God's word challenges and corrects this concept of God. The Bible says God created man in his own image, but modern man has returned the favor: We have created God in our image…a pleasant friend, but not one who inspires awe or even loyalty. We have morphed him into someone who is dedicated to meet our needs, but who doesn't require much from us. The awe-inspiring Almighty God worshipped for centuries has become a "cosmic good buddy" or a personal servant whose job is to make us happy. In his book, *Reaching for the Invisible God*, Philip Yancey quotes an observation by Doris Lessing. She noted that many people think it's God's job to jump into our lives and make us feel better: "Jehovah does not think or behave like a social worker."[6]

It is vitally important to hold the complete picture of God's nature in our hearts. God is wonderfully kind, tender, intimate, and attentive. He is a friend, but he is an

---

5   Larry Crabb, *Finding God*, (Zondervan, Grand Rapids, 1993), p. 18.

6   Philip Yancey, *Reaching for the Invisible God*, (Zondervan, Grand Rapids, Michigan, 2000), p. 132.

awesome friend! His power is unimaginable. His hold on creation is unshakable. His holiness burns with such an intense flame that sin is consumed in his presence. If we have even the slightest glimpse of his majesty, we, like the apostle John, will be so overwhelmed with his greatness that we'll faint at his feet (see Revelation 1:12-18). The truth is, the more I understand who God really is, the more deeply I worship him in awe!

Spirit and truth—full devotion and an accurate understanding of God's character—both are essential to be fully alive in Christ. Suppose that my wife Marie told you, "I adore Rick because he has this full head of thick, curly blonde hair" (Which hasn't been true for a number of years now!) How do you think I would feel about her compliment? And she may continue, "I love my husband because he's the best fix-it man on the planet. Give him a hammer and a screwdriver, and he can fix anything!" If you know me well, you know that I can barely tell which end of the hammer to use, so Marie's comments would make you wonder if she knows me at all. Those comments would not help our relationship. I would wonder who she was talking about. But instead, she may tell you, "I adore Rick even though, to be honest, his hairline is trying to run away from his forehead. And even if he can't fix a single thing around the house, I still love him." This expression of affection in the context of an honest and accurate appraisal will deepen the bond of relationship between us, and it will ring true with you. It's the same way with God. He has given us the insights of his word to help us understand what he is really like. By reading, studying, and talking about the truths of the Bible, we gain a more accurate concept of the nature of God. As we find out more about his mercy and purpose, our hearts are filled with him, and the gnawing emptiness is shattered by his presence. Our passions are inflamed by one who loves us so much, and worship seems like the only reasonable response.

SUNDAY MORNINGS

I became a Christian when I was in the oil business, and on Sunday mornings, I was completely focused on God. The worship service was, quite frankly, the highlight of my week because it reminded me of God's grace and greatness. During that hour, I felt my heart was completely, totally, absolutely devoted to Christ. But then Monday happened, and stress, demands, deadlines, needs, and schedules almost instantly distracted me. Day after day, I came home tired. Marie and I were busy raising kids, trying to make our marriage work, and tending to the myriad of things that are part of American life. Gradually through the week, all of Sunday's heartfelt devotion to Christ leaked out of my life! By the next weekend, I felt drained, and I desperately needed the Sunday worship service to pump me up again.

To be honest, it used to bother me that I was such a hypocrite, so devoted to God on Sunday, but so distant from him by Friday. A few years ago, we attended a Rich Mullins concert. He was one of my favorite songwriters and recording artists, but is now in heaven. At the concert, he talked about his frustration with being focused on God one minute and totally oblivious to him the next. He shared his frustrations with some friends, hoping they would give him encouragement. One of them told him bluntly, "You hypocrite! Why don't you quit going to church on Sunday? Just quit being a hypocrite!"

Rich responded, "That's the *only* hour of the week that I'm getting it right, so I'm not about to quit going. For that one hour, my thoughts are focused on God and my heart soars. As for the rest of the week…I think I'm beginning to do better. My experience of God's presence is beginning to last a little longer through the week. No, I'm not about to give up that hour on Sunday. I might give up the rest of the week, but I am not going to give up that hour of worship."

Sunday morning at church is not the sum total of worship, but it's essential to a life of worship. God told Moses, "You may work for six days each week, but on the seventh day all work must come to a complete stop. It is the Lord's Sabbath day of complete rest, a holy day to assemble for worship. It must be observed wherever you live" (Leviticus 23:3). God not only wired us so that he alone can fill the hole in our hearts, he also wired us to need the seventh day to reflect on his character, enjoy his people, and rest from all our work. We need one out of every seven days to refuel spiritually, to gather together

> *We need one out of every seven days to refuel spiritually.*

for encouragement, and to "get it right" for that one hour. If we miss two or three Sundays, spiritual drift begins. That's just the way we're wired.

Many people equate singing with worship. Certainly, singing can be a part of a life of worship, but the two are not synonyms. Listening to the message is also an act of worship, if we listen intently, reflecting on the points being made, and looking for ways to apply the truths we learn. It might be tempting to think worship stops when the offering basket is passed, but that's not the case at all. As we've seen, true worship is responding to God's character in full devotion to him. Because he has rescued us from a tragic eternity and has given us the most wonderful gifts imaginable, we respond by gladly giving him all of our time, talents, and treasure. When the offering basket comes around, we have yet another opportunity to worship God. Giving out of guilt or a sense of obligation would not be an act of worship. Paul reminds us, "For God loves the person who gives cheerfully" (2 Corinthians 9:7). So that my giving doesn't just become mere habit, when the offering basket comes around, I often silently say, "Jesus, I'm giving because I adore you so much. I worship you."

Sunday morning isn't limited to what happens during the service. Before the hour begins and after the hour is over, greeting one another can be an act of worship. Even though we may be tired from a long week, we can look beyond our own needs to extend a handshake or a friendly "hello." We can ask about someone's day, and we show love even though we may not know the person. We may see someone we don't even like, and we can choose to worship God by showing kindness instead of being cold to that person. Do you know the delight the Father has in that act of kindness? That's exactly what he did for us when we were cold to him!

Every moment of Sunday morning can be an act of worship for each of us. In this hour, we connect with God and with the community of faith. As we are refueled spiritually, the impact of this hour can linger long after we have exited the parking lot. Even if we feel like a hypocrite the rest of the week, God invites us to "come as we are" and worship him on Sunday mornings in the community of faith. For that one hour, we can get it right!

24/7

Worship is not just for Sunday mornings. God wants our affection and loyalty 24/7, all day every day. More than once, I've asked myself why

> *Worship is not just for Sunday mornings.*

people like me tend to think of worship as an event instead of a lifestyle. There might be several reasons. One is that we do "the church thing" for an hour on a specific day of the week. Centuries of tradition have drilled it into our minds that we worship on Sunday morning for that hour. We are also event driven. We think things are important if and when they center on a specific time and place, and especially when a lot of people gather for the event. And finally, our concept of worship might be limited because we simply don't grasp the foundational point that we live and breathe under the leadership of Jesus Christ all day every day. Too often, we give him a little attention for an hour each week, like a tip to a waiter. But the fact is, all we are and everything we have comes from his hand. The more we grasp his goodness, the more we'll want to honor him with every word and action. The more we understand his wisdom, the more we'll depend on him for every decision at home, at work, and everywhere we go. The more we sense his greatness, the more we'll trust he can work in every situation, large and small.

Paul taught the believers in Rome about God's forgiveness, majesty, and purpose, then he told them how to respond. He wrote, "So brothers and sisters, since God has shown us great mercy, I beg you to offer your lives as a living sacrifice to him. Your offering must be only for God and pleasing to him, which is the spiritual way for you to *worship"* (Romans 12:1 NCV). Paul's tone was inviting, not demanding or finger-pointing. In the previous chapters, he had just described the goodness and grace of God with more clarity than ever before. In light of the incredible magnitude of God's love, Paul invites them to respond in the only reasonable way: by devoting themselves to God whole-heartedly and unreservedly. In light of God's mercy, that's the only response that makes sense.

It's easy to see how this kind of response shapes our attitude at church each week. We sing with more joy, and we listen more intently. But how does it affect the mundane stuff we do at work and at home? In his letter to the Colossians, Paul addressed several groups of people: fathers and children, masters and slaves. Throughout history, the most oppressed people have been slaves. In the first century, the message of Christ spread hope to every segment of society, including the slave quarters. As they became Christians, slaves then had to learn to relate to their masters in new ways. Instead of resenting their masters, they learned to honor them. Paul wrote to the slaves: "You slaves must obey your earthly masters in everything you do. Try to please them all the time, not just when they are watching you. Obey them willingly because of your reverent fear of the Lord. Work hard and cheerfully at whatever you do, as though you were working for the Lord rather than for people. Remember that the Lord will give you an inheritance as your reward, and the Master you are serving is Christ" (Colossians 3:22-24). The key to the slaves' response was to reframe their thinking. As they worked for their masters, Paul encouraged them to work hard and cheerfully, as though they were working for Christ himself. That changed everything! Instead of bitterness, they could be thankful. Instead of resentment, they could be cheerful. Their very actions of service to their masters became acts of worshiping God. Their behavior was fueled by their heartfelt reverence, adoration, and devotion to Jesus.

God's ultimate goal for us is that we will find ways to worship in every activity of our lives. Let me give you an example. We live four miles from NASA and have many friends that work with the space program. When I got the news of the Space Shuttle Columbia tragedy in February 2003, I spent many hours working with leaders at our church to communicate God's heart to people. In those meetings, my heart and mind were so clear and focused because I adore God so much. The tragedy of lost lives reminded me of how important life is—my family and friends, and especially, the eternity each of us will step into the moment life is over. That realization caused my adoration for God to soar in the midst of my grief. Even in our meetings and conversations, I worshipped him. During the day when I was alone, I was grieving, but my heart was focused on God. I prayed, "I have such reverence for you, God, because I know that in this moment of grief, we have hope in you. I know who you are, I know what you have done, and I know your love. You have given us the promise of eternity, and I'm grateful." In my time of prayer, I was fully alive with tears streaming down my face.

Every experience and every interaction can be an act of worship when it is fueled by our love for Jesus. Taking care of a sick child, making a bed,

Every experience and every interaction can be an act of worship when it is fueled by our love for Jesus.

mowing a lawn, making a corporate profit can all be acts of worship if we are doing those things with our hearts pointed heavenward expressing our devotion to him. I find the more I live this way, the more my heart soars. The more I live this way, the more fully alive I become.

THINK ABOUT IT...

1. Before you read this chapter, what image came to mind when you heard the word "worship"?

2. Read Exodus 34:14 and Jeremiah 10:8 and 11. What are some things people use to try to fill the God-shaped vacuum in their hearts? What have you used? Describe your experience: Did you find fulfillment and excitement for a while? When did you realize your substitute was going to leave you empty? How did you respond to that discouragement?

3. Summarize in your own words what it means to worship God "in spirit and in truth." (See John 4:23-24.)

4. Describe the connection between a person's concept of God and his worship of God.

5. Read Colossians 3:22-24. How does this passage apply to our study of worship? How can you apply this principle to your own life?

6. What are some applications you can make to worship more fully on Sunday?

7. What are some applications you can make to worship more fully on the other six days of the week?

FRIENDS FOR LIFE

*T*he fifth piece of the fully alive puzzle is "community." Any definition I've ever heard for the word falls woefully short. Rather than short-change you with a definition, allow me to tell you about what I have learned firsthand about this thing called community.

About twenty years ago, Marie and I experienced a truly defining moment in our lives. I had no idea how one little "yes" to a question could change the entire shape and future of two people's lives. Our life-changing "yes" wasn't strong or full of conviction. To be honest, it was half-hearted. The question someone asked was this: "Would you consider joining a small group of people that meets on Sunday morning before church?" I could easily think of a number of other things to do during that time (like getting a little more sleep), but we decided to check it out.

Our expectations were low—extremely low—as we walked into that first small group meeting. I thought we'd probably attend a few meetings, realize we were bored to death, and then stop going. (How's that for optimism?) When we walked in, Marie and I met about fifteen people. Soon we realized there was something unique about that group—something we had never experienced before.

Previously, Marie and I had attended small groups in churches, but we were turned off by a lot of religious pretense. If you didn't give the "right" answers to the questions, you were left feeling spiritually inferior and, well, stupid. We quickly concluded it was wise to avoid speaking up in those groups. After all, we didn't have a burning desire to be ridiculed and ostracized...in church, of all places. As we got to know the people in those groups, we also observed that the things we discussed on Sunday morning didn't make much of an impact on their lives the rest of the week. So these were our summary observations about small groups: To be accepted, you had to give exactly the right answers, but even those didn't seem to change anyone's life. Now you can see why our expectations were so low when we decided to attend yet another small group.

This new group, though, was radically different. They didn't care if you didn't use the right words when you talked about the Bible or God. They seemed to be genuinely glad you showed up, no matter what you said in the discussions. And as we got to know these people, we saw that they genuinely believed what they read in the Bible, and they trusted God with the smallest details of their lives. They prayed for wisdom in their decisions about their jobs, their finances, and their relationships. They read promises in God's Word and then waited expectantly for God to work. Their faith was not a "Sunday thing," but was woven throughout their daily lives. They still had struggles and questions, yet they rested in a solid faith that God would guide their lives. To say the least, their trust in God caught our attention! They lived as if God were alive and truly engaged in their lives. These people had the most attractive quality we had ever seen in people who claimed to follow Christ—they were *authentic*.

> *These people had the most attractive quality we had ever seen in people who claimed to follow Christ—they were authentic.*

I had been in church most of my life, and from my observations and experience, I had concluded that God and God's people required me to be perfect on Sunday morning. I may have had a terrible week, but as soon as I opened the car door in the parking lot, I had to put on a smile that said, "I can see you're perfect, and so am I!" None of us ever had problems, and none of us had any needs. We all had flawless families, handled money astutely, and felt close to God all the time. That artificial pretense made me sick to my stomach.

Maybe it was just me. Maybe I was the only one who was phony, plastic, and playing a role. Maybe I was the only one who sometimes felt confused about God, unsure of his involvement in my life, and clueless about how to handle difficult issues like relationships, money, and work.

The people in this new small group, though, were honest—sometimes painfully honest—about their struggles as well as their successes, their heartaches in marriage and parenting as well as answers to prayer, and their times of feeling like God was on the backside of Mars as well as moments of feeling close to him. These people were transparent, genuine, and honest. That was incredibly appealing to Marie and me!

As we got to know people in the group, an older couple won our respect. One day in the group, the husband said, "I need to be honest with all of you. We're struggling in our marriage." I was sure his next sentence would be: "And we've decided to get a divorce." But he didn't say that. To my surprise, he said, "We know that God wants our marriage to work. We're deeply committed to trying to make it work, but we need your help. We want to ask you to pray for us, encourage us, and share the wisdom of your experience with us. We need help, and we think you're the people to help us."

This dear couple would never have risked their reputations and made themselves vulnerable if the group had insisted on everybody being perfect. But in the atmosphere of honesty, acceptance, and affirmation, they felt safe to share their deepest hurts. They trusted the men and women in that group to help them through their biggest struggle. That group of people gathered around them that day and for months to come. It was a heartwarming and beautiful thing to participate in the love and support provided for that dear couple.

Week after week, we took some time in our group to listen to them, pray for them, and encourage them. Through months of ups and downs, laughter and tears, this couple emerged stronger and more committed to each other than ever before. This man and his wife weren't the only ones who benefited from this demonstration of the love of God toward each other. All of us were deeply affected.

Marie and I weren't just passive observers in this process. Watching the group support this couple with a troubled marriage gave us courage to be honest about difficulties we were experiencing, too. We had initially attended the group because we were hurting. Several months before we joined, Marie had been in her first pregnancy.

All parents know the excitement and expectations of having their first child, but well into the pregnancy, she had a miscarriage. It was a heartbreaking, life-shattering time for us. We needed a place where we were loved, where we could not only hear about, but actually experience the goodness of God. After we had been attending for a few months, Marie got pregnant again. We were delighted, yet hesitant to share our news for fear the outcome might be the same. If that happened, grieving alone seemed to be an easier path.

For weeks, Marie and I kept our secret, but as we watched the group care for the couple experiencing difficulty in their marriage, we decided to take a risk. We told them that Marie was expecting and explained what had happened in her previous pregnancy. We'll never forget their response. As soon as we told them, several people immediately said, "Let's pray for your unborn child right now." We were overwhelmed. Within seconds, the group gathered around us, and they began to pray for our baby. It was just an authentic expression of their love for us and their trust in God. We returned home that Sunday with a peace we had yet to fully understand. We sensed no matter what happened with the future of our baby, we would somehow be all right. Perhaps we were beginning to realize there was a far greater void in our lives than a child could ever fill.

As weeks went by, they asked about us and encouraged us all along the way. We began to feel more hopeful that Marie could carry the baby to term, and we felt a lot of love and support from our group of friends. I remember the day our son was born. For months Justin had been prayed for by a group of people who had no biological connection to him—but they had a spiritual connection.

Justin's birth, though, wasn't the end of the story. Marie and I lived several miles out in the country. As soon as we got home from the hospital, people in the group began bringing meals out night after night. Their drive was long, but their love was immense. After a few nights, it finally dawned on Marie and me that these people were deeply committed to us. Our commitment to the group had been minimal, but they were radically, genuinely committed to us. Watching their response to the other couple's needs had given us enough courage to share our own fears and hurts, and actually receiving their care changed our relationship with them. We were now committed to them as well. In fact, wild horses couldn't drag Marie and me away from this group! Little did we realize that God was loving us through this group of friends. He was gradually drawing us to himself. Marie remembers

Little did we realize that God was loving us through this group of friends. He was gradually drawing us to himself.

these acts of kindness as being the first time she understood unconditional love. People other than family loved her with no expectations in return.

When we met together in the group, we discussed a spiritual or biblical topic, and we always talked about what it would look like if we applied the truth in our daily experience. That was rich. Marie and I began to listen more intently, and we found time to hang out with these people at lunch after church. These people loved to celebrate! We had a blast together at parties that were good, clean fun.

During all this time in the group, Marie and I weren't too sure what to make of Jesus. We weren't Christ-followers yet, but we were fascinated by the faith of the people in the group. About ten months after Justin was born, Marie first, and then I, grasped the truth of Christ's death on the cross to pay for our sins, and we trusted in Jesus Christ. From that time forward, everything changed. I started reading the Bible each day on my own, and I was amazed at what God was teaching me through his word.

For months, people had shared their struggles and needs, and people in the group had cared for each other in all kinds of ways. Then one day, I read Acts 4:32, which says, "All the believers were of one heart and mind, and they felt that what they owned was not their own; they shared everything they had." One of the men in the group had just lost his job. He was a hard-working, bright guy, but at that point, the economy in West Texas was going down the tubes and a lot of competent people got "pink slips." For the first time in my life, my heart was filled with a sense of generosity. I realized everything Marie and I had was a gift from God, and like the passage in Acts said, it wasn't really our own. Marie and I wanted to help this man who had lost his job, and others in the group felt the same way. As a group we began to meet the needs of his family covering mortgage payments and utility bills. We were thrilled to be used by God! In the past, you would have had to beat me up and rob me to get that kind of money out of me, but Jesus was gradually changing my heart. I felt honored to be able to use my resources to help a friend and please God.

A few months later, a young mother in our group was diagnosed with cancer. She and her husband had become our good friends. She had to travel several hundred miles to Houston to M.D. Anderson for her treatment. Her schedule dictated that she needed to go to Houston at Christmas, but their strained finances couldn't pay for her husband and children to be with her. You can imagine what a group of true friends would do. We all pitched in. We bought the airline tickets, paid for the hotel bill, gave them money for eating out, and sent them off to spend Christmas as a family. Sadly, it would be their last.

Those believers described in the book of Acts lived wholeheartedly and unreservedly for Jesus Christ. Their faith went beyond their words and was demonstrated by their actions. They were so committed to each other that they sold property to meet each other's needs. They shared everything they owned. They worshiped together at the temple each day, and they met in homes for the Lord's Supper. They shared their meals with great joy and generosity, all the while praising God. As I reread this passage, I realized our group was experiencing this in our own lives! We were reliving what the early followers of Christ experienced two thousand years ago. I looked around the room at these people, and I had a clear sense that Marie and I truly had found friends for life.

After about three and half years in the group, my company wanted me to move to our corporate headquarters. We felt good about the position they offered, and in addition, we liked the perks of the promotion and a higher income. But the move meant that we were going to be ripped away from the first community of faithful friends we had ever known. As I read more in Acts, however, I realized that moving people to new places was the norm in God's plan, not the exception. In many cases, that's how his word was spread. I also discovered that the qualities of our group that we had found so attractive and life-changing were intended to be the norm for people who placed their faith in Jesus Christ.

The qualities of our group that we had found so attractive and life-changing were intended to be the norm for people who placed their faith in Jesus Christ.

Marie and I moved to Dallas, trusting that we would find or could start such a group. Within three months we found ourselves part of a fledgling, start-up small group at our new church home. Over the next five years, these people became our closest friends as we went through both the good times and the bad times of life. Since those years in Dallas, we have moved twice, first to Kentucky for seminary and then to our current home in the Bay Area of Texas. Each time we have either joined or started a small group. Each time, genuine life-changing friendships have formed.

Today, it's been more than 20 years since Marie and I walked through the doors of the small group meeting with skeptical attitudes and low expectations. Those people became, and continue to be, lifelong friends. We still see several couples from that first group. We ask about kids, vacations, and careers, and we delight in telling (and retelling) stories of "the old days." Marie and I have the same level of long-term friendships with people in the groups in Dallas and Kentucky. Now we are deeply enjoying the same kind of relationship with another small group of people.

What I've been describing is often referred to as "community." You'll find the model for it in the book of Acts in 2:41-47 and 4:32-35. Nothing is richer or more rewarding than investing in and experiencing relationships like the ones I've described. Community is a strategic piece of the fully alive puzzle. I know of no one who can experience life to the fullest without it.

THE PURPOSES OF SMALL GROUP COMMUNITIES

I believe God has three clear purposes for small groups. He intends for them to be a place where people can experience:

- Friendship that is genuine

- Care that is mutually given

- Character that is becoming Christ-like

At our church, we often refer to this as the "FCC Experience." Only in biblically functioning small groups is it likely that we will experience these three essentials to becoming fully alive in Jesus Christ.

FRIENDSHIP THAT IS GENUINE

The first purpose is for a group to be a place where *friendship is genuine.* Solomon knew a lot about relationships. He observed, "A man of many companions may come to ruin, but there is a friend that sticks closer than a brother" (Proverbs 18:24 NIV). God created us with a desire and a need for close relationships. We may have a thousand superficial relationships ("many companions"), but those do not meet our needs. We need people that we can "do life with," that will be committed to us through thick and thin—people with whom we can celebrate, with whom we can laugh, and with whom we can grieve. We need people who can truly know us and still love us. Without such friendships, life can be lonely. Solomon went so far as to say that without rich, close relationships, we ultimately "come to ruin." As we learned in West Texas, the "friend that sticks closer than a brother" is usually found in these small groups. Their lives become expressions of "Jesus with skin on."

CARE THAT IS MUTUALLY GIVEN

God's second purpose for a small group is that it be a place where *care is mutually given.* Solomon wrote, "A friend is always loyal, and a brother is born to help in time of need" (Proverbs 17:17). For all of us, the question is not *if* crisis will come. The question is *when* it will come. On our darkest days, we need friends who gladly shoulder part of the burden as if they were "born to help in time of need." We also have the need to be that kind of friend to others.

God's intent is for the small group to be the *primary care unit* of the church. This works well for three reasons:

- In a healthy small group, friends will quickly become aware of needs that arise, making it possible to provide immediate and timely support.

- In a healthy small group, help can be provided by the very people who care the most about the person in need. Caring for someone you love is almost an instinctive response.

- In a healthy small group, *everyone* is a care-giver, so burnout due to care-giving should be rare. If a church doesn't see small groups as its primary care unit, a few compassionate but over-committed people try to meet the needs of far too many. In that model, burnout is inevitable.

Over the last 20 years, I have seen small groups rally around hurting friends in every imaginable way. I have seen their continual presence in hospital rooms during a long-term illness. I have seen them provide meals, child care, and lawn maintenance when a family faced crisis. I have seen them provide comfort and incredible friendship to a grieving spouse. I have seen them meet every critical financial need imaginable. I have seen lives that are fully alive in Jesus Christ.

I know of a man who unexpectedly lost his job, and with it, his company car. After his small group encouraged him and prayed with him, one in the group pulled out his car keys and said, "I know you'll need a car this week to look for a job. This car is yours for the next week." Another in the group pulled out his billfold and gave him a handful of cash—all he had, saying, "This will help put some food on the table." The next week the same scene was played out: prayer, the loan of another car for a week, and cash for expenses. Later, the man who had lost his job told me with tears in his eyes that he had never experienced the love of Christ as he did in his small group during those two months when he went without work. The only ones more impacted were the care-givers in his small group.

CHARACTER THAT IS BECOMING CHRIST-LIKE

The genuine friendship and mutual care-giving that we can experience in a small group are priceless. God has a third purpose for our groups. He intends to *grow the character of Christ in us* as we "do life together." In the simple act of caring for one another, we become more like Jesus. When we notice others' needs and take action to help them, the character of Christ is built in us just a little bit more that day. We understand a little more of his heart of love, and we learn to put others' needs in front of our own desires.

> *In the simple act of caring for one another, we become more like Jesus.*

The Bible gives us instructions for how our groups can shape our character: "Think of ways to encourage one another to outbursts of love and good deeds. And let us not neglect our meeting together, as some people do, but encourage and warn each other..." (Hebrews 10:24-25). *Encouragement* and *warning*—two things I desperately need from true friends. Countless times when my faith and energy are fading, encouragement from our small group has infused me with strength and hope for the week ahead. I have yet to meet a person who truly thrives spiritually without the encouragement of friends.

I also need friends who will warn me when they see me drifting off course. Years ago in Dallas when our boys were little, Marie and I were part of a small group. I was extremely busy with career, church involvement, and the needs of a growing family. One night one of my best friends in our small group, Mike Lang, pulled me aside. He simply said, "Rick, your boys will only be young once, and they need your best." Though his words hurt, I listened, because I knew Mike was a true friend with my best interests at heart. Because of Mike's words, I realigned my priorities as a father, a realignment that's still in place today. My sons' lives have been deeply impacted because this friend in a small group cared enough to "warn" me. King Solomon wrote, "As iron sharpens iron, a friend sharpens a friend" (Proverbs 27:17). That is the role we can play for one another in small groups.

TWO COMMITMENTS

To become a member of a small group, only two things are required: *time* and *love*. Most groups meet once a week for an hour or two; some groups meet every other week. All of us find time for the things we truly value, and after reading this chapter, I hope you can see enormous value in being a part of a community of faith. Many contemporary writers have observed that busyness is a great enemy of relationships.

> *To become a member of a small group, only two things are required: time and love.*

If we are too busy, we simply can't have rich, significant relationships. Strong, vibrant relationships are the greenhouse for spiritual growth. God didn't design us to be spiritual Lone Rangers. He created us for community, and we grow when we are linked closely with others who love and follow Jesus Christ.

The second commitment is to love the people in the group. Let's be honest, they won't be perfect, but then neither are you and I! We will need to love them for who they are. That's how Jesus loves us, and his plan is for us to become more and more like him. Love is not a feeling—it's a choice. It's a unilateral commitment that isn't based on the qualities of the one we choose to love. But love doesn't come out of a vacuum. John tells us that we love others out of the wealth of our experience of God's love for us. He wrote, "God showed how much he loved us by sending his only Son into the world so that we might have eternal life through him. This is real love. It is not that we loved God, but that he loved us and sent his Son as a sacrifice to take away our sins. Dear friends, since God loved us that much, we surely ought to love each other" (1 John 4:9-11). And when the love we have experienced from God is poured out in relationships with people who become "closer than a brother," watch out! Exciting things happen in individuals, the group, the church, and the community.

Let me make this perfectly clear. The message of this book is about the unmitigated thrill of becoming fully alive in Christ, but I don't believe we can achieve that fullness of life unless we are in close connections with others who are on the journey with us. In these relationships, faith grows as we share our greatest hopes and deepest hurts, pray for each other, search for direction from God's word, and worship God for his goodness and greatness with people who become our closest friends.

As you recall, Marie and I first joined a group with only a half-hearted "yes," but that experience changed the course of our lives. You may have a million reasons why you don't want to be a part of a small group: Your spouse won't come, your children have soccer practice, you travel a lot and would have to miss some gatherings, you're too tired after work, you don't want to miss your favorite television show, or something else. The question is not: Is it perfectly convenient to join a group? The real question is: In light of the promises of God to use small groups to sharpen you and help you grow in your faith, which group should you join? If you join a group and it doesn't appear to be a good fit, consider staying another week or two to give it your best shot. If it still doesn't work for you, find another group. In other words, don't stop looking until you find a group of friends like Marie and I found. We wouldn't think of trying to do life without a small group. I hope you won't either.

THINK ABOUT IT...

1. Have you been a part of small groups in the past? If so, describe your experiences.

2. Read Proverbs 18:24 and write the verse in your own words. What do you think it means to "stick closer than a brother"?

3. Read Proverbs 17:17. Describe a time when you were in need and it seemed that nobody cared. What did that experience do to you? Describe a time when you were in need and a person or a group of people came to your assistance. What happened through that experience in your life and in your relationship with those people?

4. Read Hebrews 10:24-25. The passage says to "think of ways to encourage one another to outbursts of love and good deeds." What are some ways you can encourage specific people in this way?

5. Read Acts 4:32. If you are in a group at this point in your life, how can you help move the group toward more of an Acts 4:32 experience?

6. If you aren't in a group, what benefits could you experience from being in one? How can you find out more about the possibilities for being in a group? After reading this chapter, are you committed to find one? Why or why not? What is your next step?

CHAPTER

6

A STUNNING FREEDOM

Several years ago, a man called to make an appointment with me. A few days later, we met after work. He told me honestly, "I'm genuinely struggling with questions about faith in Christ. I'm not sure if I can really believe all this stuff about him. I think it's time for me to see if what people say about Jesus is true—or not." He could tell I was happy to hear he was exploring the relevance of Christ, so he continued, "First, I'd like to find out if Jesus was a man who really lived at a time and place in history. And if he lived, did the Romans actually nail him to a cross? That would be really significant, but the next question is the really difficult one. Is it possible that Jesus died on that cross and then actually came out of the grave alive?" He paused for a second, then he asked, "Rick, would you talk to me about that?"

I was thrilled, and I told him, "I'd be glad to talk about those things." We began to talk that night about the historical record regarding Jesus of Nazareth, and we met almost every week for many months. I gave him *The Case for Christ* by Lee Strobel and suggested some other books, and he studied the issues. One evening many months later, he looked at me and said, "After reading and studying, I've come to the point that I really believe all this about Jesus. I believe he was the Son of God."

In my mind, I thanked God for the privilege of walking beside him on this journey. I had been more of a spectator than a guide. Occasionally, I offered him a little direction and encouragement in his search, but in most of our meetings, I just sat and watched God work in his life. Silently, I told God, "This is the biggest thrill I could ever have!"

The silence and my gratefulness were broken by his words: "I believe Jesus is the Son of God, but Rick, I'm not sure that I want to follow him."

> *"I believe Jesus is the Son of God, but Rick, I'm not sure that I want to follow him."*

His statement stopped me dead in my tracks. I stammered, "Would you explain that to me? I'm afraid I don't understand."

He sighed deeply, then he continued, "I'm clear about this: If I become a follower of Christ, there are certain ways he wants me to live. If I follow him, I'll have to give up the good life *now* in order to get the good life *in heaven*. Isn't that the deal? The trade off in becoming a Christian is to diminish the quality of my life now in exchange for a higher quality life in heaven." He looked straight at me and said solemnly, "I'm not sure if I'm ready to make that trade."

To be honest, I shouldn't have been surprised at his reluctance to follow Christ. Many people come to a rational conclusion about who Jesus is, but they are challenged by the implications of actually following him. Many years before, I had faced the very same challenge. I had the same thought process, and I came to the same hesitant conclusion. After listening to the message about Christ, I believed that I had to give up the best life now in exchange for the best life in eternity. The thoughtful but discouraged man sitting in front of me had made the same mistake I had made years before. Neither of us had understood the real message, the real offer, and the real hope promised by Christ.

After thinking about his words for a few moments, I told him, "It's obvious that you've been reading the Bible because you've understood that God wants you to live in a different way. You may have read Peter's statement in his first letter. He wrote, 'But now you must be holy in everything you do, just as God—who chose you to be his children—is holy' " (1 Peter 1:15). I explained, "Holiness is simply doing things God's way. I know you realize that's part of following Christ." I paused to see if he understood what I was saying. He nodded, so I continued, "But there's another part. Jesus told his followers, 'The only reason I came

> *Holiness is simply doing things God's way.*

was to give you life in all its fullness. I came to make you fully alive.' " After pausing a second, I looked him in they eye and asked, "Well, which is it? Does God demand that we be holy, or has he promised to make us fully alive and give us the most satisfying life we can imagine?"

I waited for the question to sink in. His previous statement assured me this was exactly the problem he was considering, and I knew giving him a quick answer wouldn't cut it. After a few seconds, I told him, "This is one of the most important questions anyone can ask, and I appreciate your honesty in asking it. Would you like to keep meeting so we can explore this issue?"

Over the next several weeks, we talked about Christ's offer to make us fully alive and God's demand that our lives be changed. At one point, I asked him, "How do you think God might diminish your life if you follow him?"

He was very candid. He paused a second, then said, "The issue is integrity. It's very clear to me that God wants me to have integrity in every aspect of my life. I have some friends and business associates who get ahead by cutting corners, and I don't see how I can compete with them unless I cut corners, too."

That helped clarify the issue. I thought for a second, then I told him, "I'm quite a bit older than you. Let me tell you what I've seen." I told him some stories about people I had known in business who cut corners to gain an advantage. In almost every case, these people enjoyed some initial gains, but sooner or later, they paid dearly for their lack of integrity. As I told him these stories, the lights seemed to come on. He knew people, too, who had ruined their careers and their reputations by dishonest business practices. Each of them initially had made a lot of money or been promoted quickly, but eventually their deception was exposed, and their lives were wrecked.

A week or so later, he shifted to a different objection. He related, "I read in the Bible that God wants sex to be experienced only within marriage. And from what I've read, he wants even my thought life to be perfectly pure. I look around at some of my friends. They sure don't live that way, and they seem to be having a blast. Rick, that's giving up a lot!"

We were now getting to some issues that were way beyond intellectual questions about the resurrection! I told him, "On the surface, it looks like having as much sex as possible with as many people as possible is the epitome of life. But what happens as the years unfold? What are the consequences of sexual exploits?" We talked some about the damage and emptiness that accompanies promiscuity. Sooner or later, the excitement of the chase and the thrill of secret sexual encounters result in broken marriages, angry and distant children, health problems from STDs, and the shame of ruined reputations. But at the height of anticipation, those costs aren't figured in the pro forma! I also told him of the people I know who struggle in their present marriages because of the relational and emotional damage inflicted by sexual activities before they married.

As I answered one set of questions to his satisfaction, he moved to other areas of life. We talked about the inherent but deceptive promises of drugs, gambling, and the unbridled pursuit of possessions. Each time, I related stories of men and women who believed these promises, and for a while, experienced excitement and satisfaction. Eventually, though, all of these promises went unfulfilled, and lives were often shattered in the process. I summarized for him what I had learned from my personal experience and from

Sin always derails our pursuit of being fully alive.

my observations of others. Sin *always* derails our pursuit of being fully alive. It *always* diminishes our lives. It *always* leaves us in a ditch. There are no exceptions.

Our conversation so far felt like a cost/benefit analysis of a balance sheet. These facts were true, but they were sterile. I explained to my friend that when I began to trust in Jesus, a relationship was established with God. This relationship is so close the Bible describes it as "Jesus living in me," as Paul wrote in Galatians 2:19-20. At any time I can turn my attention toward God and find his welcoming presence. The writer of Hebrews describes it this way: "So let us come boldly to the throne of our gracious God. There we will receive his mercy, and we will find grace to help us when we need it" (Hebrews 4:16). King David found this relationship with God to be of such personal importance that he wrote, "But as for me, my contentment is not in wealth but in seeing you and knowing all is well between us" (Psalm17:15 TLB).

I explained to him that when I sin, my relationship with God becomes strained and uncomfortable. I'm still forgiven, Jesus still lives within me, and I can still turn to God at any moment. The problem is, I have trouble looking God "in the eye." I avert my gaze when I'm in his presence because I know "all is not well between us." I know I have somehow hurt him by my thoughts and actions. I still have a relationship with God, but it's strained.

I gave him an illustration from my college days. I was living at home the summer before my senior year. I had worked the previous summers far from home and had forgotten that my routine of staying up late greatly differed from my parents' schedule. The first few days at home I stayed out late with friends. After a few nights of this, at supper one evening my father reminded me that they had to get up early for work and, in our small home, when I came in late, it would wake them. He asked me to be home by 11:00 P.M. on weeknights. I agreed.

A few nights later, I was out with friends when 11:00 P.M. rolled around. We were having such a good time I decided to "make an exception" to our recent agreement. I didn't get home until 1:00 or 2:00 in the morning. The next evening at supper, I couldn't look my dad in the eye. All I could do was stare at my food. I knew I had disappointed my parents. I knew I had failed to live up to our agreement and had made their day difficult. I was still my parents' son, they still loved me, and I was still welcome at their table. But our relationship remained strained for several days until I was willing to say, "I'm sorry I broke our agreement. I know I disappointed you and hurt you. I really don't want to do that again. I plan to be in by 11:00 each night."

When I told this illustration to my friend with all the questions, I said, "The relationship had been hurt by my bad choice, but after I told them I was sorry, everything was good between us again." Then I connected the dots. "It's like that between us and God. As a follower of Christ, when I sin, he is offended, I feel guilty, and I can't look him in the eye. I don't have to guess if there's a problem be- tween us—there's a ten-ton weight on my shoulders! That is a heavy price to pay for doing things my own way! If you do things God's way, if you choose the path the Bible calls 'holiness,' then you experience a life of freedom. In fact, it's a stunning freedom! You can live life richly and deeply, communicate with God and look him in the eye because everything is good in the relationship. And every aspect of life is affected positively: family, friends, work, fun…everything."

I could tell my friend was thinking hard. I completed the thought for him. "If you'll choose this path of follow- ing Jesus, you'll discover an unbridled freedom. You'll learn how to become fully alive."

My friend and I talked for a few more months, then one night he told me, "Rick, I've known for some time that Jesus is God the Son, but as of tonight, I want to begin following him." That night, he began a relationship with Christ, and he started experiencing the incredible freedom that comes from loving God and following his path. Is that path "holiness" or "freedom"? The answer is "yes"; it's both at the same time. The choice to walk with God in truth and grace brings incredible freedom to be the people God created us to be. It's not a swap of giving up pleasures in this life now for pleasures in heaven later. God has created us so that we experience the greatest fulfillment and satisfaction now by walking with him. And none of us can even imagine what the pleasures will be like in the next life! Stunning freedom is the result of making good choices to follow Christ. *Holiness—simply doing things God's way—*is the next piece of the puzzle as we learn to be fully alive.

BUT HOW?

Living a life of holiness requires a partnership between God and us. As Paul writes, "You are partners with Christ Jesus because of God. Jesus has become our wisdom sent from God, our righteousness, our holiness, and our ransom from sin" (1 Corinthians 1:30 GWT). There's no way we can be fully alive and live in the stunning freedom of holiness on our own. We don't have enough wisdom and strength, and we would focus far too much on selfish purposes instead of God's. We simply must have God's help.

> *God gives us the ability to live holy lives. It's not something we can do on our own.*

God's part

In his first letter to the Corinthians, Paul told them, "The Lord has now set you free from the awful power of sin." The main point of this verse is that it is God who gives us the ability to live holy lives. It's not something we can do on our own.

God does two significant things to equip us to live in stunning freedom. First, the moment we begin to follow Jesus, he gives us a new heart and a new spirit, both of which are, in their very nature, good. Ezekiel talked about this when he wrote, "I will give you a new heart and put a new spirit in you. I will remove your stubborn hearts and give you obedient hearts. I will put my Spirit in you. I will enable you to live by my laws, and you will obey my rules" (Ezekiel 36:26-27 GWT). A fundamental change takes place at the core of our being. Our spiritual DNA is changed. Before, we were "bent" toward sinning, but now, we are "bent" toward holiness.

The second thing God does when we put our faith in Jesus is place his Holy Spirit within us (see Romans 8:9). His Spirit gives us both wisdom and power: the wisdom to make good choices and the power to act on those decisions. Before we trusted Christ, we did the best we could do on our own. But now we have the motivation as God's dearly loved children and the wisdom and strength of his Spirit to make choices that please him and benefit others and us. I frequently pray, "Lord, I know that your Holy Spirit in all of his wisdom and power is living within me. I yield my thoughts, my words, and my actions to your Spirit. Guide me and give me the strength to do your will in this circumstance."

In Philippians, Paul wrote, "For God is working in you, giving you the desire to obey him and the power to do what pleases him" (Philippians 2:13). From the time you began placing your faith in Jesus, through all the days up to now, at this very moment, and for the rest of your life, God is working to give you the desire to obey him and the power to please him. That's an incredible truth, but that's only half of the relationship.

Our part

We aren't lifeless robots that God somehow activates to make us do things. We aren't puppets; we're partners with God in the challenge to change lives—including our own. Let's look at six elements of our responsibility as partners with God.

1. Ask God to show you what he wants changed in your life.

People who are serious about following Christ are well aware that they aren't perfect. In fact, as they get closer to the flame of God's love, his light exposes the stained places in their hearts more clearly. In the first months of knowing Christ, we become aware of the big and gross sins, but as we grow, God shines his light into the hidden crevasses of our hearts. There, previously hidden impurities, such as jealousy, apathy, and bitterness, are exposed. None of us escapes the light of exposure in the eyes of God. In a beautiful poem about God, King David began by acknowledging that God's eyes see everything: "O LORD, you have examined my heart and know everything about me." And he ended this psalm with an invitation for God to reveal absolutely anything that might come between them. He pleaded, "Search me, O God, and know my heart; test me and know my thoughts. Point out anything in me that offends you, and lead me along the path of everlasting life" (Psalm 139:1, 23-24). On a regular basis, each of us needs to ask God, "God, what is it you want changed in my life? Please show me."

Sometimes I ask God to show me what he wants to change in three specific areas of my life: my relationships, my work, and my thought life. My heart's desire is to find where I'm out of line, because those things hinder my closeness to him and my experience of freedom. Someone may read these words and think, *Wow, Rick must be really dense. Can't he tell when he's messing up?* The answer to that question is: Sometimes I can, and sometimes I can't. It's so easy to drift along thinking a behavior or an attitude is perfectly fine, simply because those actions and thoughts have become ingrained in my life. The prayer at the end of David's psalm is simply saying, "God, I don't trust myself to see everything in my life, but I trust you to let me know if something's wrong."

A friend of mine had been a Christian about four years when we saw each other one autumn afternoon, and he told me, "Rick, I want to tell you something new going on in my life." He was really excited to share the news. I smiled and he continued, "About a month ago, I asked God what he wanted to change in my life." He had my attention now, and he told me honestly, "You know how much I love college football, and you know I've been betting on games for years. Gambling on college games was fun at first, but lately, I've become, well, consumed with betting. I asked God what he wanted me to change, and I felt him saying to me, 'I want you to quit gambling.' "

He was excited as he told me, "I've been thinking about it, and I realize that betting on games takes a lot of energy and a lot of time. And I get mad when I lose money. Often I end up losing both my money and my temper. That's not a good thing."

I asked him, "What did you do?"

He was really excited now. He told me, "I quit gambling a month ago. That means I haven't gambled for four straight Saturdays! Cool, huh?"

"Yes, very cool!"

As I've talked with people over the years about inviting God to show us the offensive thoughts, attitudes, and behaviors he desires for us to change, I've found that God almost always shows us only one or two things at a time. Our spouse or our teenager might fill an entire notebook with their list of things we need to change, but God graciously focuses on one or two at a time. I appreciate that. When we make changes and develop new habits concerning those, he moves on to others when he—and we—are ready.

2. Repent—make a 180-degree turn.

It's not enough to know what's right and wrong. We have to take steps of correction. To repent means "to turn and go the other way." So when God shows us something to change, we say to him, "I'm sorry for offending you in what I've been doing. As of this moment, I want to turn away from it and go the other direction." In David's confession about his sins of adultery and murder, he knew it wasn't enough just to feel sorry for what he'd done. He asked God for the courage to obey him. He wrote, "Create in me a clean heart, O God. Renew a right spirit within me.... Restore to me again the joy of your salvation, and make me willing to obey you" (Psalm 51:10, 12).

On some occasions, I've tried to make a 120- or 170-degree turn away from an offensive attitude or behavior, but that doesn't work very well.

To go in the opposite direction is to make a 180-degree turn. On some occasions, I've tried to make a 120- or 170-degree turn away from an offensive attitude or behavior, but that doesn't work very well. (I know this sounds a lot like an engineer trying to explain spiritual truth, but stay with me!) When I try to change only part of it, or I've tried to see how little I could change, it just doesn't work. Let me tell a story that explains what I mean.

When I was a kid growing up in South Texas, we had a mesquite tree in our front yard. Throughout the summer, my brother and I ran barefoot around our yard and the neighborhood. Several times in the course of each summer, my brother and I would step on big, thick mesquite thorns, driving them deep into our bare feet. We screamed, ran (or limped) to the house, and my mother got her tweezers to pull them out. Let me fill you in on a little botanical insight about mesquite thorns. The top part always came out very easily, but often, the point broke off inside our feet. After a few painful attempts, she would give up and sigh, "When your dad gets home, he'll take it out." My mother didn't have the stomach to endure all the screaming. Sooner or later, dad walked through the front door, mom told him about the buried thorn, and he would say, "Come over here, son. I have to take this out, because if I leave the tip in there, it'll get infected—then there'll be a big price to pay. So sit right here. We're going to get the tip out right now." And he always did. (I'll spare you the painful details.)

The same principle applies when we need to turn away from destructive thoughts or behaviors. In effect, God says to us, "Here's something I want you to change, and I want you to change it completely. I don't want you to keep part of it, and I don't want you to toy with it. If you leave the tip in, it's going to cause all kinds of problems. It's better to deal with it completely and immediately." Repentance is the second responsibility in our partnership with God. We say, "God, I'm sorry. I'm going to turn and go the other way."

3. Guard your mind.

In our partnership with God, we trust him to work in the recesses of our hearts, but he also works in our thoughts. Paul encouraged the believers in Rome, "Let God transform you into a new person by changing the way you think" (Romans 12:2). Every action begins in our minds, and I'm certain that every sin I've ever lived out began with a thought rambling around in my head. I entertained that thought, let it develop into a seemingly plausible plan, and eventually I acted out that plan. It seemed reasonable, but I was deceived; it was actually foolish and destructive. Paul encouraged the Romans and us to change the software in our thought processes. Instead of letting wrong and harmful thoughts become viruses in our minds, we need to recognize them as mental spam and delete them. Don't ponder them, don't give them attention, and don't analyze them. Delete them.

One of my good friends from seminary moved to one of the wealthiest communities in America. He told me that a lot of people in his church have mansions. He and his family live in a nice house, but one of the challenges for him is a nagging sense of envy about others having more than he has. He told me, "My wife loves to look at model homes, and she really enjoys looking at the biggest, prettiest, most expensive ones she can find. That's when it really gets me. We'll look at these model homes, and as I'm wandering into the seventh bedroom the thought suddenly hits me, 'I should have this. In fact, I deserve this! Why should somebody else have it?' It's just a downhill spiral from there to self-pity, anger, and resentment." He explained, "It doesn't take a rocket scientist to figure this out, but I've had to stop looking at model homes. I just don't go there. I simply have to guard my mind. I know where the thoughts of envy and dissatisfaction come from, and I don't even want to have to fight those thoughts, so I just don't go there." He smiled, "I have one less problem to deal with now. When envy occasionally visits, I remind myself how blessed we are with the home we have."

He was smart. He was "guarding his mind" from the source of his envy and greed. In a similar way, you and I can "guard our mind" by avoiding the sources of temptation in our lives.

4. Fill your mind.

After guarding our minds from wrong and destructive thoughts, it is important to replace them with God-honoring thoughts. What should we focus on? The writer to the Hebrews tells us, "Let us strip off every weight that slows us down, especially the sin that so easily hinders our progress. *We do this by keeping our eyes on Jesus*, on whom our faith depends from start to finish" (Hebrews 12:1-2). To fill our minds with constructive thoughts, we first rivet our minds on Jesus. His presence gives us courage, his wisdom gives us clarity, and his love gives us hope. I find that merely thinking about his very real presence within me helps me to live this life of holiness.

What else do we focus on? Paul gives us this practical wisdom: "Fix your thoughts on what is true and honorable and right. Think about things that are pure and lovely and admirable. Think about things that are excellent and worthy of praise" (Philippians 4:8). There are innumerable practical ways to help us "fix our thoughts." Marie has put scripture verses on our refrigerator and on light switches around the house as reminders of God and his goodness. A friend of mine tapes scripture to the handles of his lawn mower to prompt his thoughts as he does yard work. For the last 19 years, I've worn a ring that bears a cross and a fish as a constant reminder of the One I follow.

I don't know about you, but I need to remember that what fills my mind has a direct bearing on how closely my thoughts, words, and actions line up with God's best for my life.

5. Ask a friend to help.

As you have seen throughout these pages, the Christian life isn't meant to be lived alone. To be fully alive in Christ, we need each other. The fifth element of our responsibility is to ask a friend to help us live out this life of freedom. Solomon wrote of the importance of support: "A person standing alone can be attacked and defeated, but two can stand back-to-back and conquer. Three are even better, for a triple-braided cord is not easily broken" (Ecclesiastes 4:12). It helps to have a friend who understands. This friend should be one you can trust and who won't share any confidences outside your friendship. It needs to be someone that deeply loves you, will

Look for a friend who will pray for you, challenge you, and hold you accountable.

root for you to do the right thing, and will speak boldly when you wander off course. Look for a friend who will pray for you, challenge you, and hold you accountable. Feeling helpless, confused, and alone crushes our spirits. A friend can help us stand strong.

6. When you fall, get back up and go to #1.

No matter how far we travel on the path of following Christ, we fall from time to time. When we fall, we need to get back up, go back up to #1, and start over again. One of my favorite passages in the Bible is Lamentations 3:23, which says, "Great is his faithfulness; his mercies begin afresh each day." Each day— in fact, every moment— God's mercies are fresh for us to start again. And so when you and I fall, we need to get up and say, "God, I'm sorry I've offended you, but I want to make a 180-degree turn. Help me start again."

A few years ago, I watched one of the most exciting bowl games in college history. The Fiesta Bowl was the site of the National College Championship, pitting Miami against Ohio State, two undefeated teams ranked #1 and #2 in the polls. Ohio State won the game in double overtime. After the game, I saw my friend who had quit gambling. I asked him, "How'd you like the game?"

He laughed and said, "I can guarantee that I had a better night than you did!"

Instantly I reacted, "Oh, you must have bet on Ohio State." Then I realized what I'd said, and I told him, "That comment wasn't very sensitive. I'm sorry, I forgot you quit gambling."

He smiled and told me, "Let me tell you what's happened since we last talked about my gambling. We got into the holidays, and all the NFL playoff games and college bowl games were being played. An old friend called me and said, 'Hey, you want to place a wager on this game coming up?' I thought, 'Oh, what the heck, it's no big deal.' So I placed a bet on the game. Like before when I bet, I got all wired and excited about the game. But the next day, I talked to God, and I said, 'God, I know this isn't what you want for me!' I told God, 'I'm sorry. I'm going to do a 180 again. God, you said you don't want me to gamble, so I'm not going to do it any more.' "

He had a grin on his face now as he continued his story, "On the night of the Fiesta Bowl, I was going to watch the game and have a great time, even though I had placed no bets. Then I noticed my kids really wanted my attention. A year ago, I would have sent them to another room. I would have gotten into the game and shouted and yelled and screamed, and maybe cursed if my team was losing, but I said to my kids, 'Let's go rent a couple of movies and watch them tonight!' That's what we did. They wanted to set up some tents in the living room, so we made tents out of sheets draped over the sofa and chairs. They wanted some popcorn, so we popped a couple of bags. It was the best night of my life with my kids!" With the biggest smile I've ever seen, he told me, "So Rick, I don't care how much you enjoyed the Fiesta Bowl. I had a better night than you did!"

I shook my head and laughed. I told him, "I think you're right. You sure did!" I've watched this friend for several years since he quit gambling. Just like me, he still has a long ways to go to do everything God's way, but he's doing more God's way every day. With every good choice, I see his eyes getting brighter, and I see his steps getting lighter. I see him looking into the eyes of everyone he meets, with nothing to hide. Now he can say to God, "God, my contentment is in seeing you and knowing all is well between us." He's learned what the psalmist wrote, "I have gained perfect freedom by following your teachings" (Psalm 119:45 CEV). His heart's cry is, "From this moment forward, my heart's desire is to do everything in my life the way God wants me to do it." That's a life of holiness. That's a life of stunning freedom.

THINK ABOUT IT...

1. Before you read this chapter, how would you have described or defined "holiness"?

2. Which best describes your perspective?

    —Doing things God's way means giving up "the good life."

    —Doing things God's way is "the good life."

    Explain your answer.

3. When you look at times you've done things God's way, was your life enhanced or diminished? Was the ultimate outcome good or bad? How about when you haven't done things God's way?

4. Read 1 Corinthians 1:30. Give a synopsis of God's part and our part in living in stunning freedom, and describe the roles of each "partner."

5. Read Philippians 2:13. What are some ways God "is working" in you and in other Christians who are truly following Christ?

6. Review the six responsibilities for our part, then describe at least one specific thing you can do to apply each one to your life today:

— Ask God to show you what he wants changed.

— Repent—make a 180-degree turn.

— Guard your mind.

— Fill your mind.

— Ask a friend to help.

— When you fall, get back up and go to #1.

7. Read and paraphrase Psalm 119:45.

A Test of Faith

*M*oney will play a significant role in determining how fully alive you become. Although you may readily agree with that statement, you may be surprised to read it here, so let me say it again: Money will have a considerable impact upon the degree to which you experience this "life to the fullest" that Jesus came to give you. But here is the counterintuitive part. The quality of your life will not be determined by the *amount* of money you possess, but rather by how you *manage* whatever amount is in your possession.

It's tempting to think that a little more (or a lot more!) money will take our lives to the next level. Who among us hasn't dreamed of winning the lottery or receiving an inheritance from a rich uncle we never knew existed? Who among us hasn't considered how much better off we would be if we could only increase our income by 20%? We don't necessarily crave a lot of money; we just think we need more than we have.

I'm a casual student of American capitalism, and I enjoy reading about the industrial giants of the ages. Some of the icons of capitalism have made very telling statements about money. Railroad tycoon W.H. Vanderbilt, who built the lavish Biltmore Estate near Asheville, North Carolina, said, "The care of two million dollars is enough to kill anyone. There is no pleasure in it." Vanderbilt, however, never stopped pursuing wealth. John Jacob Aster made millions in real estate, including building the Waldorf-Astoria. Before he died in the sinking of the Titanic, he stated, "I am the most miserable man in the world." In the early part of the 20th century, John D. Rockefeller made a fortune in the oil business. As the founder of Standard Oil, he became the richest man in the world. A reporter asked, "Mr. Rockefeller, what will it take for you to be happy?" He answered, "Just a little bit more. Just a little bit more." Steel magnate, Andrew Carnegie observed, "Millionaires seldom smile." Henry Ford built one of the biggest businesses in the world, but he reflected, "I was happier when I was just a simple mechanic." Each of these individuals possessed an enormous amount of money, yet found their wealth did not make them any more fully alive. Neither will any amount of money give us the life we really want.

In contrast to these giants of capitalism, I had the privilege of closely watching a couple who grew up during the Great Depression. From our prosperous point of view today, this couple lived in abject poverty in their childhood and through the first years of their marriage. Even in the good years, their income was, at best, modest, yet they experienced genuine contentment with their limited resources. What was their secret? They learned to manage their money according to the guidelines and principles they learned from the Bible. Their money, or more accurately, the way they managed their money, enhanced their lives. I know. I watched them closely. They were my parents.

Perhaps you are like me. Perhaps there have been times you haven't managed your money wisely. You spent too much, borrowed too much, or saved too little. You know first-hand the downside of mismanaging money. You have felt the stress, the pressure, the discontentment, and the frustration surrounding your financial life. Once again, the key is not *how much* we possess, but how we *manage* those possessions. The seventh piece of the fully alive puzzle is *money management*.

LEARNING TO MANAGE MONEY

The Bible has a great deal to say about money. In fact, Jesus said far more about money than almost any other subject. In the pages of Scripture, God has given us clear guidance about money management in six key areas:

1. Earning
2. Spending
3. Saving
4. Borrowing
5. Investing
6. Giving

What we do in each of these six areas will affect the quality of our lives. There are biblical principles for each area that can successfully guide us through all of our money management decisions. There isn't space in this book to thoroughly address all six principles, so I'll focus on the area of "giving," which is the foundation of successful money management. Numerous authors, including Larry Burkett, Ron Blue, Mary Hunt, and Dave Ramsey, have written excellent books on biblically based money management that can be of help with the other five areas. In addition, the "Good Sense" financial seminar produced by Willow Creek Community Church has proven to be highly effective. Many churches around the country, including ours, offer the course on a regular basis.

A TEST OF OUR FAITH

Two decades ago, I learned that our giving is directly tied to our faith. I had been a Christian a short while, and I was up early before work spending a few minutes praying and reading the Bible. Somewhat to my surprise, I "felt" God quietly but clearly speak to me. I don't say that lightly. I am the epitome of a rational, skeptical, "prove it to me" engineer, but I had the unmistakable sense that God asked me the question, "Do you trust me?"

Two decades ago, I learned that our giving is directly tied to our faith.

Though I was a bit startled, I responded, "Yes. Absolutely, I do!"

Then I felt God say, "Then I want you to begin tithing." (Tithing means to give 10% of your income.)

Instantly, almost as a reflex, I told him, "That's different! That's not what you asked me."

I sat in the living room in silence, thinking about what had just transpired. I was certain God had spoken to me, but I was equally certain I didn't like what he had said. Marie and I were giving about two percent of our income, and I knew an increase to ten percent would be impossible! For God to connect "faith" and "tithing" was foreign to me, but it didn't take long to get the picture. To have faith in God, or to trust in God, means to follow his leading. I genuinely trusted God in some major areas: I trusted him to forgive me, to hear my prayers, and to get me to heaven. The unexpected question was, "Could I trust God with our money?" That may sound shallow and elementary to some of you, but to many of us, that's the bottom-line, gut-level test of our faith. Can we follow God's leading with our money and not end up in a ditch, regretting we ever gave up control? That morning it seemed to me that trusting God should be "all or nothing." I said to God, "Yes, I do trust you, and I'll follow your lead and begin tithing."

Then I made my first mistake. I went into the bedroom and woke up Marie. Excitedly, I told her that I thought God had just spoken to me. This was a first in our married life. She sat bolt upright in the bed, instantly wide awake. "What did he say?" she asked.

I told her, "God said he wants us to tithe."

I'll never forget her next words. With more conviction than I had ever witnessed from her, she insisted, "Well, God hasn't told me!" She lay back down with finality.

I went back to the living room where I had just been talking with God and asked, "God, did you forget to tell Marie, or did you set me up?" This time there was nothing but silence.

That night at supper, we had a rather animated debate about tithing with both of us entrenched in our opposing views. After two more evenings of similar "dialogue," I sensed God speak to me again. This time he seemed to say, "Don't rock your marriage over this. I know your heart. Let me speak to Marie." So I backed off and didn't bring up the subject again.

After several months, Marie occasionally began to bring up the subject again, and I could tell God was speaking to her. The issue of tithing had come up in her conversations with a mentor, in discussions with friends, and in a Bible study she was attending. One night as we talked, Marie raised the subject again. She told me that she now felt God had spoken to her, and she also wanted to begin tithing. We were both thrilled to be on the same page!

That very night, we sat down to see how we could rearrange our finances to begin giving ten percent of our gross income. Instantly, we hit a major problem. We were spending all that we made, and almost none of it was discretionary spending. We had a huge house payment, car payments, and other fixed expenses. Short of selling our house, there was no way to immediately begin tithing, so we decided that when I received my next scheduled pay raise in three months, we'd give the entire amount of the raise, plus whatever else was needed. That's how we'd begin tithing. We had a real sense of peace that this plan would honor God.

A couple of days later, my boss called me into his office and said I would be getting a raise three months early, effective immediately. I was stunned! I didn't know such a thing was possible with this Fortune 500 oil company where policies and procedures of an "annual" raise were so rigidly followed. In fact, during the entire 15 years I worked for this company, 10 of which were in management, this was the only case I ever knew when a raise was given ahead of schedule. Two Sundays later, Marie and I placed a check in the offering basket at church, giving ten percent of our income. We experienced a deep sense of peace and contentment in that simple act of faith.

But that wasn't the end of the story. Two days after that first tithe, my boss called me into his office again, this time to tell me I was receiving a bonus. I was shocked—it was against all odds! If you were aware of the circumstances surrounding my division, my job, and my performance that year, you would understand how utterly astonished I was. But there was my boss shoving a check across the desk. I took one look at the sizeable amount and sensed

God say, "This is the amount you would have given if you had begun tithing the first time I asked you several months ago." At that very moment, my boss asked what we were going to spend it on. He suggested that Marie and I should take an exotic vacation, but I was still in a state of disequilibrium, and I blurted out, "We're going to give it all to God." If you're in the corporate world, you know that's not the standard way to impress your boss and gain future advancement! Now it was my boss' turn to be shocked...and my turn to be embarrassed. I left his office thinking about what a fool I had made of myself. (Just a quick aside: My boss, who was a great man, began trusting in Jesus a few months later.) I sat down at my desk and did some quick math. Indeed, it was the amount we would have given had we begun to tithe from that first day God spoke to me many months before.

I went home that evening and told Marie what had happened. I explained to her that the raise was the exact amount we would have given if we'd started tithing months before. Once again, her response was words I'll never forget. She smiled and said, "Let's sit down and give it all away now before we change our minds." And so we did—every last penny.

She smiled and said, "Let's sit down and give it all away now before we change our minds." And so we did—every last penny.

There was one last surprise to the story. We were blown away by the joy we felt in giving money away. In fact, there was *no* other way we could have used that money that would have stirred such joy and contentment. There was no other expenditure that could have made us more fully alive! It would mark the beginning of a remarkable journey of trusting God with our possessions.

Two decades ago, I learned that giving is a tangible test of our faith. And I learned that God can indeed be trusted with our money.

GOD'S GUIDELINES FOR GIVING

God has given us some straightforward guidelines for giving. They're simple, but revolutionary. They aren't just about mechanically writing out a check each week. They focus on our hearts. Our beliefs about God and our attitudes about his purposes determine what we do with the resources he has entrusted to us. I want to share three basic principles for giving.

Give generously.

Solomon writes with unadorned clarity in Ecclesiastes 11:1, "Give generously." Throughout the pages of the Bible, we find this is how God gives. He gave a beautiful garden to Adam and Eve, a world-encompassing purpose to Abraham, freedom to the enslaved children of Israel, a land "flowing with milk and honey" to those who followed Moses, and forgiveness to you and me through Christ. God's generous giving is often expressed in the term "grace," which is defined as "a gift that has not been earned." Paul wrote of God's generosity, "The grace of our Lord was poured out on me *abundantly,* along with the faith and love that are in Christ Jesus" (1 Timothy 1:14 NIV). We are made in God's image, so he calls us to give generously, too.

The problem I stumbled upon was that God's definition of "generosity" differed from mine. Twenty years ago,

I considered the two percent we were giving to be very generous. I guess I was mainstream American—because that's about what the average household in the United States gives—and most of us consider ourselves to be "generous." But God considers "generosity" to *begin* with ten percent of our income. (Talk about revolutionary!) The Bible frequently instructs us to give away a minimum of a tithe. Moses wrote, "A tenth of the produce of the land, whether grain or fruit, belongs to the Lord and must be set apart, to him as holy" (Leviticus 27:30). Jesus would affirm this when he said to the Pharisees, "Yes, you should tithe" (Matthew 23:23 TLB).

It is striking to read through the New Testament and discover that every example of God-honoring giving is an example of someone giving beyond ten percent. You see Zacchaeus giving away 50 percent of all he owned (Luke 19:8) and Mary anointing Jesus with a jar of expensive perfume that most likely represented her life's savings (John 12:1-11). You see a young boy giving Jesus his entire lunch when his own stomach was most certainly empty (John 6:1-13) and a poor widow placing all she has in the offering basket (Mark 12:41-44). The New Testament message is that ten percent is merely the starting point for generous giving. It's a revolutionary and life-changing message, isn't it?

Give cheerfully.

Paul wrote to the people of Corinth, "You must each make up your own mind as to how much you should give. Don't give reluctantly or in response to pressure. *For God loves the person who gives cheerfully*" (2 Corinthians 9:7).

Marie gave me a surprise fiftieth birthday party last year. She pulled out all the stops inviting hundreds of friends for an all-out, full-meal, confetti-and-balloons celebration. She must have worked hundreds of hours to put it all together. Her gift of the party touched me to the depths of my soul. Do you know why? Because she *cheerfully* sacrificed so much to pull it off. The combination of giving so much with such a cheerful spirit told me she thought I was worthy in her eyes of a lavish gift.

When we give cheerfully to God, especially when deep sacrifice is involved, it tells him that in our eyes, he is worthy of such a gift. When Marie and I are making big decisions about giving, we take time to think through all God has done for us. We remind each other of times he has spoken to us, rescued us, provided for us, and comforted us. When we look clearly at how God has poured his grace extravagantly upon us, we *want* to give back to him.

> *When we give cheerfully to God, especially when deep sacrifice is involved, it tells him that in our eyes, he is worthy of such a gift.*

Cheerfully is the only way to give. At our church, we teach that God would rather we give nothing until we are able to give with a glad and thankful heart.

Give sacrificially.

Finally, God calls us to give sacrificially, to give beyond what we can comfortably afford from our "excess." He wants us to give to the point that we can "feel" it. He wants us to give to the point that we experience a measure of "cost."

King David understood this when he said, "I will not offer a burnt offering that has cost me nothing!" (1 Chronicles 21:24) Jesus made the same point one day about the widow who gave all she had. He and his disciples sat in the temple watching people making their donations. Luke tells us, "While Jesus was in the Temple, he watched the rich people putting their gifts into the collection box. Then a poor widow came by and dropped in two pennies. 'I assure you,' he said, 'this poor widow has given more than all the rest of them. For they have given a tiny part of their surplus, but she, poor as she is, has given everything she has' " (Luke 21:1-4).

Giving a little out of our surplus is not what God has in mind for us. One thought of the cross reminds me that sacrificial giving is what God has modeled for us.

BENEFITS OF GIVING GOD'S WAY

When we give God's way (generously, cheerfully, and sacrificially), we experience a number of benefits. I want to touch on five of them.

Giving provides us with a tangible test of our faith.

Through the years, I've found it all too easy to fool myself about matters of faith. I say that I have faith that Jesus has forgiven me and will someday give me eternity in heaven, but how do I measure that faith? How can I test it to see if it's real...to see if it's strong?

On the other hand, when I say I trust Jesus with my finances and he gives me clear instructions about giving, I have a tangible way of measuring my faith in him. When I'm challenged to give ten percent or more of an income that seems stretched as it is, I'm forced to consider whether I trust his leadership. Do I believe he is fully *competent* to guide me? Do I believe his *character* is flawless and he would never mislead me? Do I believe he has the *power* to provide for all my needs? Do I believe his *compassion* for me is unlimited and he will always lead me in the way that is best for me? (For a reminder of Jesus' leadership traits, refer back to Chapter 1.) If I indeed trust him to have these characteristics, I'll come to a point that I give generously, cheerfully, and sacrificially. If I don't trust him, I won't. It's as simple as that.

I'm grateful for anything that allows me an honest evaluation of my faith. Our giving provides us with this kind of evaluation so that we can thank him for our growth or see changes that still need to be made.

Giving reminds us that it all belongs to God.

In the second book in the Bible, Moses told the people, "But remember the Lord your God, for it is he who gives you the ability to produce wealth..." (Deuteronomy 8:18). When I graduated from Texas A&M in Petroleum Engineering, I entered the oil business on a rising tide when demand for petroleum engineers was sky high. The placement department at A&M conducts an annual survey of offers given to applicants in each field. Those of us graduating that year in petroleum engineering experienced the highest offers in the history of the university. We thought we were so talented! But the truth is, we were a bunch of engineering nerds with very few social skills. The lucrative job offers that year didn't come our way because we were the coolest guys on campus. They didn't happen because we were smarter than other students. The offers weren't made because we had family connections to presidents of major oil companies. These offers were simply gifts from the hand of a kind and generous God. Years later, I now understand that God wanted to bless us with all that money and see what we would do with it. Today, I see that everything I have is from God's hand.

David wrote, "The earth is the Lord's, and everything in it. The world and all its people belong to him" (Psalm 24:1). The prophet Haggai reminds us that God created all that we consider valuable, and he ultimately owns it. He quoted God, " 'The silver is mine; the gold is mine,' says the Lord" (Haggai 2:8). We're simply managers of the part he has entrusted to us. All of our furniture? It's on loan to us from God. Our investments and retirement accounts? On loan from God. Our salaries? That's God's money entrusted to us. Our houses? Well, the mortgage company might disagree, but God owns them, too, and he's letting us use them for a while. Every time we give, I am reminded that it all belongs to God. Every dime, every tangible possession, all of our time, and all of our abilities are owned by the Creator of the universe. He's just handed them off to us for a little while. When we give, we are giving money that belongs to him.

Giving teaches us that God is indeed trustworthy.

Money has incredible power to sharpen our thinking and force us to consider what we truly value. It's one thing to sing nice songs on Sunday or talk about a passage from the Bible, but parting with our money challenges us to see if we really believe God will come through like he promised. One of the clearest promises in the New Testament is in Paul's letter to the believers in Philippi. He wrote, "My God will richly fill your every need in a glorious way through Christ Jesus" (Philippians 4:19 GWT).

When I was in high school, a singer from Port Arthur, Texas, Janis Joplin, became very popular. The bunch I hung out with didn't sing her songs very well, but to tell the truth, she didn't sing very well, either. One of her songs had deep, rich, spiritual meaning. The chorus said (sing it with me now!),

"Oh Lord, won't you buy me a Mercedes Benz?
My friends all drive Porches, I must make amends.
I worked hard all my lifetime, no help from my friends.
So Lord, won't you buy me a Mercedes Benz?"

Let me make this very clear: That's not what God is promising. He's not saying, "I'll give you everything you want!" God promises to meet our needs, not fulfill all our wants. In the wealth and abundance of our culture, though, it's sometimes difficult to tell the difference.

Marie and I have been trusting God with our finances and our giving for twenty years now. If we hadn't begun to give this way a number of years ago, we would have missed the greatest adventure of our lives. In late 1997, Marie and I sat at a fast food restaurant talking about our future. I told her I thought God was leading us to leave a secure mainline denomination to start a new church. I openly acknowledged the huge financial risk we would be taking. We would have no financial backing, no property, and at that point, no people. All we would possess would be a vision that I believed was from God. We would only survive if God supernaturally provided. If he didn't, there was no plan "B."

> *We would only survive if God supernaturally provided. If he didn't, there was no plan "B."*

I was fully prepared for Marie to say, "No thank you. We've taken enough risks for God. I supported you when you left the oil business to become a pastor. We're safe. We're secure. Surely we've risked enough already." But Marie didn't say that. She recounted how God had *always* been faithful to us. She talked about how he met our needs when we first began tithing. She reminded me how he had provided for us through the seminary years. She looked me in the eyes and said with conviction, "Rick, for thirteen years we've trusted God, and he has provided for us every time. God has proven himself so much and so often that for us, God's faithfulness is a certainty. If he is leading you to start a new church, then let's do it. He won't let us down."

Because we had repeatedly experienced God's faithfulness with our finances, we were able to trust him again and start Friendswood Community Church. In the last several years, we've had the thrill of seeing God touch and transform countless lives. It has been the ride of a lifetime! But the truth is, we would have missed it all if we had not begun to trust God with our money back in 1985 when we began to tithe.

Giving allows us to make an investment in eternity.

When I put a check in the offering basket, I consider it a phenomenal opportunity to partner with God in the biggest, most audacious enterprise the world has ever known: reaching the planet with the good news of Jesus Christ. It is the one investment whose returns will endure forever. Every other investment Marie and I have ever made fades. Here is a current example.

Fourteen years ago we made a major investment in a minivan (they were almost cool back then—really!) Not long ago, I was driving it to a lunch appointment two miles away. In those two miles, I had to pull off the highway five times to restart the engine! My mechanic, who is a great friend because of all the business I give him, told me it would cost $2500 to repair the minivan. If I repaired it, the "Blue Book" value would be only $1500. The value of a major investment of our resources 14 years ago had "faded."

One day, everything we own—every car, every house, every new dress, every suit, every stock, and every bond—will fade. In his most famous sermon, Jesus told the crowd, "Don't hoard treasure down here where it gets eaten by moths and corroded by rust or—worse!—stolen by burglars. Stockpile treasure in heaven..." (Matthew 6:19-20 *The Message*). He was telling us to invest in that which endures. There is only one lasting investment: the investment that introduces people to Jesus and helps them become fully alive in him.

> *One day, everything we own—every car, every house, every new dress, every suit, every stock, and every bond—will fade.*

Every smart investor wants to know what kind of return he can expect. Jesus told us that if we invest in having more and better stuff, it will only be eaten by moths, rust away, or be stolen. Even if we keep it a long time, it still leaves us feeling empty as we compare it with others' stuff and long for more. But investing in eternity produces an annuity that never ends! We'll see the fruit of our giving every day for the rest of time—and beyond. Is there a better investment you could ever make? I don't want to get to heaven and say, "Oh, if I had only known, I would've invested differently, I would've spent differently, and I would've given differently." Generous giving is the only investment you will ever make that will last for eternity.

Giving increases our contentment and joy.

The Bible says, "You'll not likely go wrong here if you keep remembering that our Master said, 'You're far happier giving than receiving' " (Acts 20:35). Marie and I will never forget the day when our hearts and actions changed from giving pocket change to giving generously, cheerfully, and sacrificially. For the first time in our lives, we intentionally said, "Okay, God, we're going to trust you in this giving thing." We will remember that day because we were both blown away by the joy. The feeling was a complete surprise. A deep sense of contentment unexpectedly welled up in both of us. And now, twenty years later, we experience even deeper joy when we give.

PRACTICAL ADVICE FOR BEGINNING TO TITHE

Finally, if you have decided to begin tithing, here are some suggestions that people have found helpful.

- Pray, expressing your desire to trust God with your giving, and ask for his help and guidance.

- Develop a plan for how you will increase your giving. Don't simply increase your giving and expect it to all just work out. Determine how you will reallocate your spending.

- If you see no way to tithe today, give what you can, while prayerfully developing and committing to a plan that will result in tithing in the near future.

- Tell a trusted friend of your new commitment to tithe and ask for encouragement and accountability.

A key component of being fully alive in Jesus Christ will be determined by our *money management.* I encourage you to learn biblical principles concerning all six areas of personal finance: earning, spending, saving, borrowing, investing, and giving. And at the very foundation of biblical money management is giving. From the core of my being, I want to encourage you not to miss the benefits and the thrill of trusting God with your giving. It's a wonderful—and sometimes thrilling—ride of sensing God's leading to invest in eternal things and then taking bold steps to act on his leading. Don't miss it.

THINK ABOUT IT...

1. Have you ever experienced stress or frustration about your finances? Do you think that biblical principles about money management could help you avoid these problems and experience life more fully? Explain your answer.

2. Based upon what you have read in this chapter, describe in your own words the connection between faith and giving. What does your current giving reveal about your faith?

3. What would be your greatest concern about turning over control of your finances to God and following his principles of giving?

4. Evaluate your own giving based upon God's principles of giving generously, cheerfully, and sacrificially. What do you do well? What areas still need some work?

5. What changes would need to happen in your budget for you to give at least ten percent of your income to the Lord? Does that thought challenge you, thrill you, or depress you? Explain your answer.

6. Read Deuteronomy 8:18 and Psalm 24:1. Explain the significance in your own life of everything you have coming from God and belonging to him.

7. How can you tell the difference between wants and needs? (What would your best friend or spouse say about your explanation?)

8. Read Matthew 6:19-20. Describe the different motivations, different goals, and different outcomes of pursuing earthly treasures versus eternal treasures.

9. When have you experienced the most joy, the biggest thrill, in giving to others?

10. If the management of the money you possess is a test of your faith, what score would you give yourself? What score would God give you?

11. What is one thing you will do differently as a result of what you've learned in this chapter? When will you do it? What do you expect to happen?

CHAPTER 8

A SENSE OF PURPOSE

*A*s I look in the Scriptures, I find a foundational principle about our purpose in life. At the very core of our being, we were *created to serve.* God has hard-wired us and called us to serve both him and others. Paul wrote to the people of Ephesus, "It is God himself who has made us what we are and given us new lives from Christ Jesus; and long ages ago he planned that we should spend these lives in helping others" (Ephesians 2:10 TLB).

> *God has hard-wired us and called us to serve both him and others.*

Serving is not the role of a second class citizen in the universe. It's the role that God himself plays. Jesus tells us in Matthew 20:28, "For even I, the Son of Man, came here not to be served but to serve others, and to give my life as a ransom for many." Because we are created in his image, we will become fully alive only as we discover and step into the serving roles God has designed specifically for you and me. *Serving* is the eighth piece of the puzzle.

In serving God, we play a role in God's colossal, thrilling drama of changing lives in our homes, our neighborhoods, and around the globe. We may not be able to explain the pull we feel, but all of us long to be a part of something much bigger than ourselves. It's in our DNA to live for a transcendent purpose. There are many fine activities to which we can commit our time and energy, but the truth is, when we aren't involved in God's purpose to change lives, we miss out on a huge part of the thrilling life Jesus intended for us.

Michael Jordan's career has always fascinated me. He was one of the greatest players in the history of basketball, but at the height of his skills, he retired to play professional baseball. Playing in the minor leagues for the Birmingham Barons, Jordan applied the intensity and commitment to excellence for which he had become famous. However, in the sport of baseball, he was average at best. He never made it to the big leagues. After a year and a half, Jordan returned to basketball and was once again at his tongue-wagging, heart-pumping best. When he played baseball, he experienced mediocrity and frustration. For Michael Jordan, baseball was just a "fine activity." There's nothing wrong with the sport of baseball. It just wasn't the sport he was designed to play. Basketball was his game, and it brought out his finest skills, his most passionate determination, and his most magnificent play.

We can choose to be involved in a lot of "fine activities," but we are only at our tongue-wagging, heart-pumping best when we find the place where we can best serve God.

It's the same way for you and me. We can choose to be

involved in a lot of "fine activities," but we are only at our tongue-wagging, heart-pumping best when we find the place where we can best serve God. That place is where we are most effective, and it's also where we will be most fulfilled.

Three Truths about Serving

There are three truths about serving that I think will be both helpful and encouraging.

We each have special, God-given abilities.

As a part of our spiritual DNA, God has given each of us special talents and abilities to use for his purposes. Paul told the Romans, "God has given each one of us the ability to do certain things well" (Romans 12:6). No exceptions. Not one of us was standing behind the door when the abilities were handed out. Some of us know beyond a doubt what those abilities are, but others are a little unclear. Therefore, the first step is to identify our talents.

In four passages in the New Testament, we find lists of "spiritual gifts." (See Romans 12:6-8, 1 Corinthians 12:27-31, Ephesians 4:11-13, and 1 Peter 4:10-11.) Interestingly, these lists overlap in some ways, but each list is different. From this, we can draw the conclusion that the list of abilities God gives us is quite expansive. When we look beyond these scriptures to see how God used particular people to help others, we find an even wider variety of gifts mentioned. These include artistic talent, architectural ability, administration, banking, boat-making, carpentry, debating, designing, embroidering, encouraging, engraving, farming, fishing (Our Associate Pastor, John Wise, is going to be thrilled that I listed fishing as a spiritual gift!), gardening, hospitality, inventing, leading, managing, masonry, music, needlework, painting, planting, philosophizing, sailing, selling, tailoring, teaching, working with machinery, and almost anything else we could name.

Some gifts, like teaching the Bible, are obviously useful in the church's ministry, but *all* abilities can be used to further God's purposes. In fact, God can even use fishing. Though I have often kidded John about his fishing exploits, he uses his time, his boat, and his fishing expertise to serve others. He takes people fishing to build relationships with them, encourage them, and pour his love into their lives. Many have been impacted spiritually from these outings. John uses something as simple and fun as fishing to intentionally touch people's lives.

The key to usefulness, as well as fulfillment, is discovering your talent. As we've said, some of us are well aware of what we do well, and we can marshal our energies and time to make full use of those skills. But many of us are, at best, unsure. If we try to serve in a role that doesn't fit, two things happen, and neither of them is good: We get frustrated, and the people we are trying to serve aren't helped very much. Many of us have had the disappointing experience of giving every ounce of energy we have in an area where we are not gifted.

Years ago when Marie and I were dating, I took an eight-week woodworking class with two of my college friends. At the end of the course, they both had made beautiful, intricately crafted gifts for their girlfriends. I presented Marie with a cutting board. Eight weeks to make a cutting board! Good grief! Is it stating the obvious to tell you that it wasn't my woodworking skills that won her heart? Throughout the entire course, I was frustrated by my lack of ability, and in the end, had very little to show for my efforts. The same principle applies to how we serve. Being fully alive requires that we identify our areas of strength and then find opportunities to effectively use those abilities. When that happens, we thrive.

The best way to identify our abilities is to experiment and try different things. Most churches offer a wide variety of roles in which people can serve. Many of us find where we can serve with the most impact and the most satisfaction by the process of trial and error.

> *The best way to identify our abilities is to experiment and try different things.*

I know a young man with the ability to teach the Bible to adults. When he joined a church, he told the leaders he was willing to do anything they wanted him to do. They asked him to be in charge of the toddler class! For a year, this guy labored to connect with those little kids. Some other parents helping teach the class had a ball, but this guy almost had a nervous breakdown! As the end of the year approached, he looked forward to it like a convict longing for his release date. The day finally came, and one of the church leaders came by and said, "Thanks for working so hard in the toddler class this year. And thanks for making a two-year commitment." He had no idea that he had signed up for two years! For the sake of his sanity, he tried to find someone else to take his place, but to no avail. By the end of the second year, he was counting the days until he could be set free! This story isn't about a man who hated children. He loved children, but he only felt comfortable with a couple of them at a time. Church leaders are wise when they match the passions and abilities of people to the roles they are asked to play.

Let me give you a story on the flip side about children's ministry. Keith and Susan Earle were two of the first attendees of Friendswood Community Church. Susan tells about wanting to serve and seeing two clear options. She could either do Children's Ministry or serve on the Set-Up Team unloading our two trailers at 6:00 am each Sunday at the school we were renting. Susan said it was a no-brainer; she chose Children's Ministry. She discovered she was good at it, and she loved it. Soon after joining the Children's Ministry Team, she and three others went to a seminar at Willow Creek Community Church in the Chicago area. Susan says, "It changed my life, and it changed the entire way we looked at children's ministry. At Willow Creek, they emphasized how fun and exciting it's supposed to be, and they taught us a new way of teaching. The training was fantastic!" Susan finds such a sense of accomplishment and satisfaction in serving in the Children's Ministry that two years ago she left her career in public education to become Director of Children's Ministry at our church. Susan discovered her God-given gifts and is using them to serve God with a joy that spills over to hundreds of children and dozens of volunteers. Using our God-given gifts makes all the difference.

Everyone plays a vital role.

Paul understood that every follower of Jesus has a crucial part to play in accomplishing God's purposes. Some are more visible than others, but each is essential. To make his point, Paul used the human body as a metaphor of the church, which is sometimes referred to as "the Body of

Christ." He wrote, "But God made our bodies with many parts, and he has put each part just where he wants it. What a strange thing a body would be if it had only one part! Yes, there are many parts, but only one body. The eye can never say to the hand, 'I don't need you.' The head can't say to the feet, 'I don't need you' " (1 Corinthians 12:18-21). Paul concludes by saying, "Now all of you together are Christ's body, and each one of you is a separate and necessary part of it" (1 Corinthians 12:27).

Several years ago, I met a man named James Bond Lewis. Mr. Lewis was about 80 years old and lived in a veteran's center. I really enjoyed talking with him, so I dropped by to visit him from time to time. He had a great personality, and he loved sports, so we always had a lot to talk about. One day I went to see Mr. Lewis, but he wasn't in his room. I stepped out into the hall and saw him approaching in his wheelchair. I raised my hand to wave to him, and at that instant, to my horror and shock, his leg fell off and he ran into it with his wheelchair! It took a few seconds for my brain to process what had occurred, but after a

> *To my horror and shock, his leg fell off and he ran into it with his wheelchair!*

moment of abject horror, I realized that Mr. Lewis had an artificial leg. As I stood in the hallway trying to absorb this new information, a nurse walked by, casually picked up his leg, put it on his lap, and said, "Here's your leg James Bond. You don't need it 'cause you're just going to get in bed."

Mr. Lewis looked up at her and said, "Excuse me, Missy, but without my leg, I can't get into bed!" I left that day with a fresh appreciation for each part of the human body, and a renewed grasp of the importance of each and every part of the body of Christ. *Each* of us plays a vital role in fulfilling God's plans.

One Sunday morning a few years ago we parked a car at the front entrance of the building, took off one tire, and left the car supported by three wheels and a jack. That morning we talked about how that car had three out of four tires actively engaged in doing its job. But of course, unless all four tires were in place, the car would be going nowhere. All four tires had a vital role to play. It was an easy connection to talk about the church. Three out of four people serving with their God-given abilities isn't enough. The God-honoring potential of the church will never be reached unless *all of us* serve in the capacity for which God designed us. Everyone has a vital role to play.

Our churches were never intended to have a "football strategy" of involvement. At the college game Marie and I recently attended, there were 22 tired people in the game desperately in need of rest, while 75,000 of us sat in the stands desperately in need of exercise. God has designed us all to be "on the field" playing our hearts out for a cause that will echo through all eternity.

I have a crazy dream of every person who is a Christ-follower getting involved to serve in some way or another. I'm convinced that's God's design. Imagine how a community would be transformed by just one such church! If only a few are serving, a few great things can happen. But if all of us value the abilities God has given us by taking action to serve, God just might move mountains. As pastor and author Vance Havner once said, "A single snowflake is frail and inconsequential, but when enough of them stick together they can stop traffic."

No one is disqualified.

Rick Warren related a time when he opened his Bible at random, and almost everywhere he turned, he found men and women who were used by God to accomplish incredible things. That's not a surprise. The shocking thing, though, is that each of these people had a major character flaw, ones that would seemingly disqualify them from serving God. Abraham was too old. Jacob was a deceiver. Leah was, well, not pretty. Joseph was abused and betrayed by his brothers. Moses stuttered. Gideon was poor and timid. Samson was incredibly strong, but he was too fond of the ladies. Rahab was a prostitute. David committed adultery and murder. Elijah was depressed. Jonah was jealous. Naomi was a poor widow with nothing to offer. John the Baptist was about as odd as anybody who ever lived. Peter was impulsive. Martha was a worrier. The Samaritan woman had been divorced five times. Zacchaeus was unethical and selfish. Thomas doubted. Paul made himself the chief enemy of Christians before he came to faith himself. All of them had enormous character flaws, but God used each one to play a vital role in his plans.

That's encouraging! If you and I think we just don't cut it for some reason, we need to remember this list of rogues God has chosen to use. In fact, if we don't have a deficiency, we won't treasure God's grace and power in our lives. That

> *We need to remember this list of rogues God has chosen to use.*

was the problem with the Pharisees. They thought they had it all squared away, so they didn't appreciate God's great grace. Their rejection of grace stood in the path of them being used by God. It seems, then, that the only people God can't use are those who don't see a need for his forgiveness, love, and power to transform their lives. All who consider themselves to be sinners and everyone who is hurting can apply—these are the ones God uses. In fact, the only thing that disqualifies you is if you permanently quit breathing!

Peter wrote, "And *all* of you, serve each other in humility" (1 Peter 5:5). That includes you and me.

SEASONS

It is important to realize that there are some seasons in life where it may be best *not* to serve within your local church. These seasons tend to fall under one of three categories:

- A season of unusual demand on your time and energy. Perhaps you've just had a baby, or someone in your family is suffering from a severe illness and needs special care. Of course, in these times you're still serving, just in a different capacity.

- A season in which pain or grief is nearly debilitating. In these times, you might need to simply receive ministry and care from others.

- A season of exhaustion. This can happen when a person has been serving intensely for a long time. At times like this, rest and renewal are necessary to help you once again be at your best.

These seasons are almost always temporary. If you find yourself in one of these times and sense the need to step back for a time, don't hesitate to do so. It can be best for you and for those you serve.

The Deal

In one of the most memorable conversations in the Bible, Jesus explained his values to a group of people. Jesus called the crowd and his disciples together to listen to him, and he said, "If you insist on saving your life, you will lose it. Only those who throw away their lives for my sake and for the sake of the Good News will ever know what it means to *really* live" (Mark 8:34-35 TLB). Jesus was saying to us, "If you try to cling to everything you can grab, it will fall through your hands like sand. But if you gladly respond to my love and trust me with your life, instead of grasping for more, you'll love to give yourself to others. That's what it means to be fully alive!" If we focus on ourselves, *we lose.* If we focus on serving Jesus and his cause, *we win.* We really live!

Many things promise to fill our hearts, make us happy, and give us thrills. These things, though, are like sand in our hands. We grasp for more, but the grains seep out until we have nothing left. But our life with Christ is exactly the opposite. Instead of Christ always demanding more but leaving us feeling empty, he fills our hearts with love, peace, and wisdom. We are satisfied—deeply satisfied—and we delight in helping others find hope and healing, too. When we met Christ, there was no greater thrill than finding out we were forgiven and loved by him. Now that we are his, there's no greater thrill than partnering with him to touch people's lives.

Where Do I Start?

If serving God is new to you, here are some practical steps you can take:

1. Pray, expressing to God your desire to serve him. Ask him to guide you to a role that will best honor him.

2. Show a friend the wide variety of spiritual gifts listed in this chapter (see pages 167–168) and ask what they see you doing well.

3. Find out what serving roles are available at your church. Select one that you think might fit your interests and abilities.

4. If the role you select isn't working out well, speak with your ministry leader about trying a different ministry.

5. When you find a role that fits your interests and abilities, look for training and development opportunities that will maximize both your skills and your impact for God's work.

6. Enjoy your service for God. Bask in it. It's what you were created to do!

NO GREATER THRILL

A few weeks ago, we had a Vision Sunday at our church. We spent the morning focusing on where we have been and, more importantly, where we believe God wants us to go. The most powerful part of the morning was a five minute video put together by our Creative Director, James Baker. The room went dark, and with the soft sound of water gently splashing, these words began slowly scrolling up the screens:

"Over the past 365 days...

we've sung 1000 songs together,

set out 1000 parking cones,

made 1700 pots of coffee,

changed 2500 diapers,
made 2300 shuttle trips to offsite parking
traveled 8000 miles on student ministry trips
served 41,000 cookies,
set up 50,000 chairs,
and volunteered 27,500 man-hours.
Why?
For the 85 people that were buried on May 1, 2005 (a long pause)
And then raised to a new life."

Just as that line appeared, the stirring sounds of "The Wonderful Cross" by Chris Tomlin filled the auditorium. Then video footage of our last baptism began to roll. The images of brand new followers of Jesus being baptized blended with images of the cheering crowd of hundreds who had come to celebrate the event. Superimposed on the screen, 85 names slowly scrolled before our eyes. The video concluded with these words:

"For you were buried with Christ when you were baptized. And with him you were raised to a new life because you trusted the mighty power of God, who raised Christ from the dead"
(Colossians 2:12).

You could almost "touch" the presence of God in the room. Later in the day I talked with several people who said, *"That's* why I do parking ministry!" *"That's* why I serve in the nursery!" *"That's* why I lead a small group!" *"That's* why I'm part of the audio visual ministry!"

Friends, being invited by God to play a role in introducing people to Jesus—to be invited to play a role to help them become fully alive—is the greatest thrill imaginable! You were made for that thrill. Don't miss it. You'll find yourself becoming more fully alive!

THINK ABOUT IT...

1. Describe a time when you felt great about helping other people.

2. Read Ephesians 2:10. What difference does it make to realize that God has given you talents and abilities to use to help others?

3. What are the things you do well? What activities give you energy? What activities drain you? What activities give you a lot of enjoyment and fulfillment?

4. Are you currently doing any of these fulfilling activities in connection to Christ or the church? Explain your answer.

5. Read 1 Corinthians 12:18-27. Think of people you know in the church, and assign a part of the body to represent each one's contribution. Which part represents your role? Does that encourage you or discourage you? Explain your answer.

6. Read 1 Peter 5:5 and the section in this chapter about "no one being disqualified" from serving Christ. Describe the impact of people who think they have no need for grace, and describe the impact of people who have experienced God's grace.

7. What's the next step for you? Where will you get information about getting plugged into a meaningful role to serve God? How will you know if a role fits you or not?

THE HEART OF JESUS

hen our boys were much younger, Marie and I took them to the beach for a long weekend. That Saturday was one of those beautiful "chamber of commerce" days. The sun, sand, wind, and waves were perfect. The boys and I played for hours in the surf on an inflatable raft. Eventually the boys tired out, and Marie took them back to the beach house for some rest. I was enjoying the beach so much I decided to stay and soak up the beauty of the day.

After a while, I noticed a man in the distance walking down the beach toward me. As he got closer, I could see he had "athlete" written all over him. You know the type: chiseled muscles, great tan, confident stride…full head of hair. It was disgusting! My first thought was, *Yeah, but I'm sure he has a lousy personality.* My second thought was, *I'm sure glad Marie isn't here!* You know—she was spared the pitiful sight.

About the time he approached where I was sitting, Mr. America veered off and walked into the surf. I didn't pay much attention to him for a while, but when he caught my eye again, he was past the second sandbar where the bottom dropped off sharply. Suddenly, I did a double take. It looked like he was struggling in the water. I shook off the thought. After all, this man had the look of an athlete. I squinted so I could see more clearly. He was definitely thrashing about, but I couldn't imagine him not being able to swim. If he was just horsing around, someone sure would look silly trying to save him. It didn't look like he was calling for help, but he sure looked desperate. As the man went completely under the water for the second time, there was no longer any doubt that he was drowning!

I looked down the beach. There were no lifeguards—nobody close at all. Instinctively, I knew I should go in after him. Thoughts were racing through my head at warp speed. *He's not asking for help…I'm really not a very good swimmer…What if I go in after him and he takes us both down…I have this inflatable raft I could use…what if in his panic he tips it over drowning us both…I have a family to think about…the risk is too high!* For the life of me, I can't explain what happened next.

I simply turned and walked away. Just like that, I turned my back on him and walked back to my safe, comfortable life.

I got perhaps fifty paces toward the beach house and came to my senses. I turned, ran back, grabbed the raft, and I charged into the water.

IF YOU HAD BEEN THERE

If you had been on the beach that day, what would you have done?

If you had been on the beach that day, what would you have done? You may have wrestled with doubts, you might have been afraid, but you would have charged into the water! A life was at stake. You would have thrown caution to the wind and put your own life in harms way. You'd never walk away from a drowning man...would you?

A PARABLE

The story you have just read didn't really happen. Well, it actually did happen, but it happened in a different way. You see, what you read was a parable of an event that occurred in my life a number of years ago. Parables often help us see the familiar with fresh perspective. Parables can wake us when we've been lulled to sleep by the routine of our lives. Candidly, this parable speaks to an area of our lives where most of us are, at best, sleepwalking. Let me tell you the story of what actually happened.

When I worked for a large oil company, I hired a young engineer who I'll call Jake. He was a prize recruit who had "success" written all over him. He worked in several of our locations his first few years before I brought him into my group in our headquarters. Jake excelled in every role he had undertaken, and by now was a polished professional. He had the rare combination of excellent technical and people skills. He had incredible fashion sense and could have graced the covers of *Forbes* or *GQ* with equal ease. Jake had loads of money, drove a Corvette, and often had a beautiful girlfriend on his arm. If he tired of her, he could find another in a heartbeat. Jake "had it all."

One day, Jake received word that his father had suffered a massive heart attack and had died almost instantly. The blow was sudden and unexpected. Jake left the office for a week or so to bury his father and be with his mother. As the only child of a close-knit family, his grief was intense.

During this same time in my life, I was experiencing significant spiritual growth. For the past six years since I had begun to follow Jesus, I had gotten up early each morning to spend time praying and reading the Bible before going to work. That time of prayer had gradually become much more personal. At first, it was so personal that it almost seemed irreverent. I would sit down to pray and simply start with, "Good morning, Lord. How are you this morning?" Then I would sometimes follow with, "What's on your heart today?" As time went by, I became more comfortable with the knowledge that God wants our conversations with him to be as intimate and "everyday" as that.

One of those mornings, I asked God the question, "What's on your mind today?" and I felt God respond.

Though there was no audible sound, I had a clear sense that God answered, "A drowning man is on my heart today. It just so happens, you know him. He's in your world. His name is Jake."

Instantly, I had the unmistakable sense that God wasn't talking about Jake drowning in grief over the loss of his father. He was drowning spiritually. God was reminding me that Jake was living a life apart from him. He was living without God's forgiveness, his leadership, his power, and his comfort. That morning, I sensed that God was telling me, "If Jake goes on this way without me, he'll have a tragic, godless eternity—he's a drowning man." As I thought about this conversation with God, I knew what he was directing me to do. In an instant, I felt the Holy Spirit tell me, "Rick, I want you to tell Jake about Jesus."

And of course, I instantly obeyed God and the very next day told Jake how I had come to know Jesus and how he had changed my life. That's what we do when someone is drowning, right? Well, not exactly. To be painfully honest, I informed God that Jake wasn't asking for help, and I had learned long ago that giving unsolicited advice wasn't a good idea. That, I thought, was the end of it. I got up from my prayer and went to work without another thought about my conversation with God.

The next morning, I started my prayer the same way, "How are you, God? What's on your heart today?"

Immediately, I felt God say to me with even more passion, "There's a drowning man on my heart, Rick. His name is Jake."

I stammered for a minute, then told God, "Well, let's be honest. I'm not very good at telling people about Jesus. I'm really not. In fact I don't know how to even begin the conversation. I'll be awkward, and I'll blow it. I'm sure that's not what you want, Lord." That, I was convinced, was an irrefutable argument. I finished my prayer, got up, and went to work.

The next morning, God and I started our conversation the same way again, and in a flash, God reminded me that Jake was a drowning man on his heart. My arguments weren't making much of a dent in God's attitude, so I tried another angle. I told him, "I'm not sure if it's a good idea for me to tell Jake about Christ because there's a lot at stake here. You see, he works for me. We have a professional relationship, and everything is going great right now. I sure don't want to mess that up, and I'm sure you don't either." Again, I felt that my reasons were good, so I left for a day at the office.

Weeks went by, and as I kept asking God what was on his heart, I felt the intensity of his love for Jake burn more

I was closer to God's heart than I had ever been, but I was discovering that I couldn't stay there if I remained cool to the things that mattered most to him.

brightly. My time with God in the mornings was becoming uncomfortable. I was closer to God's heart than I had ever been, but I was discovering that I couldn't stay there if I remained cool to the things that mattered most to him. I could see a choice coming. I would have to back away and gain a little distance from God's heart and his passions, or I would have to begin caring about what he cared about.

During those weeks, I heard a song on the radio by Charlie Peacock. I liked the song so much that I bought the tape. To my surprise, there was another song on the tape titled, "Drowning Man." That caught my attention, so I put the tape in and played it. This is what I heard:

"You don't ask a drowning man if he wants to be saved
When you know he's sinking down,
Down beneath the crashing waves.
Betrayal wears two faces, both easy to explain.
One is what you say and do to bring another human pain.
When you refuse to act, though you know the good to do,
When you refuse to speak what's right, you've worn the face of number two."[7]

---

7   "Drowning Man," *The Secret of Time*, Charlie Peacock, Sparrow Records, 1990.

The chorus says that you don't ask a drowning man if he wants to be saved. If you see him in trouble, you take action to save him. That's an important point—one that addressed my first reason for not talking to Jake about Jesus. But the song continues and describes two types of betrayal. One is overt. We all know that's wrong. The second kind, "the face of number two," is more easily excused but just as painful. That type of betrayal occurs when we know someone is in need but we fail to help. The message of that song hit me like a sledgehammer. Every time I put the tape in, that song played. God was speaking to me.

After a little time, I decided to talk with Jake. To be honest with you, my decision had nothing to do with feeling like I *should* talk with him. I simply didn't want to go back to a less personal, more distant relationship with God. I had found that growing intimately close to God's heart, knowing what mattered most to him, and being challenged to align my heartbeat with his was so rich I didn't want to give it up. So one morning, I said to God, "Lord, I'm going to talk with Jake about you, but I need your help. I don't know how to transition the conversation in a way Jake will most likely hear me. I could just jump in, but I think he would put up some barriers."

I sensed God saying, "You make plans to talk with him, and I'll give you the transition."

The next day, I invited Jake to lunch. We went to a restaurant that had about a hundred tables. As we looked at our menus, there were several times that I almost blurted out everything I'd ever learned about Jesus, but each time I caught myself. I thought, *No. God said he would provide a transition. I'll just sit tight and watch for him to work.* We ordered, and soon the salads came. Again, I was tempted to just jump right into the subject of Christ, but I forced myself to wait. The main course was served, and a moment later, a man sitting at the table next to us grabbed his chest and fell to the floor. He was having a massive heart attack! The place went nuts! Waiters came to help the man. Somebody called 911. A moment later, paramedics barged through the door and ran to the man lying near us. They quickly administered aid, put him on a stretcher, and carted him off to the ambulance.

The entire restaurant sat in stunned silence. In the silence, I felt God say to me, "Now, Rick. Jake's heart is ready."

In the silence, I felt God say to me, "Now, Rick. Jake's heart is ready."

I'm certain that God didn't cause that man's heart attack to help me start a spiritual conversation with Jake. But I am equally certain that God knew what was going to occur at that precise time, at that specific restaurant, at exactly that table. Of the hundreds of restaurants we could have gone to, of the hundred tables at which we might have been seated in that restaurant, God made sure we were at that specific table. There could not have been a more gripping circumstance for my friend. His father had died of a heart attack just weeks before, and now he watched helplessly as another man faced life and death. God put us at the place and time of his choosing. I looked at Jake and said, "I've told you before that I'm so sorry about what happened with your dad." He nodded his acceptance of my heartfelt compassion. Then I said, "I'm sure you've heard about Jesus."

He replied, "Yes, of course."

I asked, "Would you mind if I tell you about what Jesus means to me?" He smiled and nodded his approval, so I told him how I had come to faith in Christ and that Jesus offers to forgive our sins and give us new life. He asked questions, and we talked for a long time.

Jake didn't place his faith in Jesus at lunch that day, and I'm not sure if he has even now. Not long after we talked, the company transferred him to another office. Before he left, we had a few more conversations. At one point, he told me he appreciated all I had told him about Jesus, then he said, "Rick, I'm convinced Jesus is a great teacher, but I'm not sure about him being the Son of God." I explained to him that if Jesus claimed to be God but he wasn't, he was either a lunatic or a liar. That would disqualify him from being a great teacher. The only other option is that he told the truth when he said he was Lord, God in the flesh. Jake understood the logic of what I was saying, and I gave him a Bible. I turned to the passage in John's gospel when Jesus told people, "I am the way, the truth, and the life." Jake was thinking about things. He asked, "How do you know it's not all superstition?"

That was an easy one. I looked him in the eye and told him, "Jake, you know me really well. I'm an engineer. You know I make you turn over every single stone in every analysis for the company. That's what I did when I analyzed Jesus. Can I show you some of the stones I turned over?" We talked about the deity of Christ, the historical record of the resurrection, the statements about Jesus made by Roman and Jewish historians, and lots of other things that support the claims of Christ as the Son of God.

Jake moved on to his new assignment, and before long, God directed me to go to seminary to prepare to be a pastor. When I resigned from the company, the first call I received was from Jake. He said, "I still don't know about

Jesus, but now I know you're willing to risk everything because of him. You really believe this."

On the average, people hear about Jesus from seven different people with whom they have significant contact before they become Christians. I was one "link in the chain" of contacts in Jake's life. My prayer is that at some point, Jake has, or will, become a follower of Jesus. Until that time, Jake is still a drowning man.

> *On the average, people hear about Jesus from seven different people with whom they have significant contact before they become Christians.*

Just in case you haven't guessed it by now, the ninth and final piece of the fully alive puzzle is *evangelism.* The word literally means "to tell good news." In our case, evangelism is simply telling people the good news about Jesus Christ and inviting them to trust in him.

THE HEART OF JESUS

Looking back, I'm not surprised that God's heart was on a "drowning man" that morning years ago. That's where God's heart always is. Recently, as I was reading through the Gospels (Matthew, Mark, Luke, and John), I was struck by the consistency of Jesus' heartbeat. With every sunrise, Jesus' heart was beating for someone whose relationship with the Father had been broken. With every sunrise, his heart was stirred for someone who was still outside God's Kingdom. Jesus thought so much about these people, he even coined a new term for them. He called them "lost" people, people that had lost their way, people who would be lost for all eternity unless something changed.

With one sunrise, you see Jesus' heart for a few lost, uneducated fishermen (Matthew 4). He reached out to them and invited them to follow him. Another sunrise, his heartbeat was for a wealthy, prominent man named Matthew who cheated his neighbors (Matthew 9). Jesus offered him a new life and a restored relationship with the Father. Another day, you see Jesus making the long trek from Judea to Galilee. He chose an unusual route because his heart was focused on a foreign woman whose life was in ruins (John 4). She had been through five marriages and was currently living with a man, but Jesus went all this way just to extend to her the love and grace of the Father, and he offered her a new beginning.

With yet another sunrise, Jesus crossed the Sea of Galilee to the region of the Gerasenes because his heart beat for an insane man who lived among the tombs (Luke 8). Everyone else avoided this man like the plague, but Jesus made a difficult journey to find him. Jesus healed him both mentally and spiritually, giving him a new life—one that won't end. On one sunrise, his heartbeat was for a common criminal who would be executed that very day (Luke 23). Jesus' attitude was: *There's only one last chance to reach him. I'll take a cross on my shoulder and carry it up Skull Hill. I'll let them drive stakes through my hands and my feet. If I let them hang me up there beside him, I'll have one last opportunity to save this lost man.* And once again, Jesus saved a lost, drowning person.

The Bible speaks often of heaven and hell, explaining that they are real places where real people will spend eternity. It is no exaggeration to say that heaven is described as "other worldly," a place where there will be no more "death or sorrow or crying or pain" (see John's description of heaven in Revelation 21). In contrast, Jesus frequently warned that hell is a place of "outer darkness, where there will be weeping and gnashing of teeth" (Matthew 8:12), and the place "where the worm never dies and the fire never goes out" (Mark 9:48). In essence, Jesus said repeatedly, "Don't go there!" He made it his mission to change the eternal addresses of drowning people.

Some of us feel uncomfortable with the concept of hell. Jesus' clear perception of hell, however, compelled him to go to the cross to rescue drowning people. In his book, *Seeing and Savoring Jesus Christ,* John Piper observed, "The word 'hell' is used in the New Testament twelve times— eleven times by Jesus himself. It is not a myth created by dismal and angry preachers. It is a solemn warning from the Son of God who died to deliver sinners from its curse. We ignore it at great risk."[8]

Is it any wonder that when I asked God what was on his mind that morning several years ago, he placed on my heart a drowning man who was very much within my reach, a man I saw five days a week? *With every sunrise,* Jesus heart is focused on "drowning" people, on "lost" people, people who don't have a relationship with the Father. And it's God's dream for us that we might become more and more like Jesus (Romans 8:29), that we might think like *he* thinks, we might feel what *he* feels, and we might do the things *he* would do if he were in our shoes.

---

8   Piper, *Seeing and Savoring Jesus Christ,* (Crossway Books, Wheaton, Illinois, 2001), p. 125.

Allow me to be personal and specific. God's dream is that you and I would begin to care deeply about the spiritual lives of others. He wants us to genuinely care about the lives and the eternities of people around us who don't know Jesus. With every sunrise, he wants our hearts to beat in unison with his own for his "lost" children. If this becomes our heartbeat, it will be natural that we will begin the adventure of introducing people to Jesus Christ. Evangelism is the ultimate adventure. In evangelism, we become fully alive!

> *God's dream is that you and I would begin to care deeply about the spiritual lives of others.*

RELATIONAL EVANGELISM

I once thought that evangelism was done only by Billy Graham and trained pastors, so I was surprised to learn that 85-90% of all Christians point to a friend or family member as the greatest influence in their decision to trust in Christ. In other words, it's almost always through close and trusted relationships that people consider Jesus and begin to follow him. This means that there are some people in your circle of contacts—family, friends, neighbors, co-workers, classmates—that no one can influence spiritually as well as you can.

In my early years as a Christian, I had very little idea of how to help someone come to faith. Maybe it will help if I summarize for you what I have learned.

Develop a "Top 3"

If I focus on "saving the world," I can easily feel overwhelmed and not do anything. But if I focus on two or three people in my circle of contacts, then I can be specific about how I connect with them and pray for them. I ask God to show me two or three in whose lives he may want to use me. These become my "Top 3."

Pray

With every sunrise, pray for your "Top 3." Ask God to work in their lives and draw them to himself. Ask him to use you to help them in their spiritual journey. Recently, I was looking at an old prayer journal. That particular year, I was consistently praying for seven men to trust their lives to Jesus. As of now, five of them have. God works powerfully through prayer.

Next steps

Each week, ask God what your next step is in these relationships. It may be a step to grow the friendship, such as going to lunch or pursuing a mutual hobby. It may be a more direct spiritual step such as asking about their spiritual background or inviting them to church. As busy as most of us are, I find if I'm not intentional about planning the "next step," it might not ever happen.

Stay the course

On the average, a person will be a "seeker" for 1 1/2 to 2 years before making the decision to trust in Jesus. Walk alongside people throughout this time—through the highs and lows of life. You never know when an opportunity might arise to point them toward Christ. Don't try to rush things, and don't lose focus. We need to be in it for the long haul. There's a lot at stake!

FULLY ALIVE

When are you most fully alive?

Fifteen years ago I was working as Director of Acquisitions for a large oil company. I had just proposed to our president and executive council that we make a major acquisition from Meridian Oil Company. The group agreed and asked who might have contacts at Meridian to begin our discussions. Surprisingly, none of us had contacts, so we were all told to look through our files for any possible connection.

Returning to my office, I was surprised to find a note that Hunter Malson had called. Hunter was one of my closest friends in college, but we had lost track of each other through the years. The note said Hunter worked for Meridian Oil Company! It was a terrific break. I assumed Hunter could tell me who we needed to contact at his company. When I called Hunter, I learned to my surprise and good fortune that he was Chief Engineer of the entire company. His boss was the person my company needed to meet with, so we set up a lunch in Houston. I lived in Dallas at the time.

At our scheduled lunch, before we had even finished our salads, it became apparent that Meridian had no interest in selling. We still had a lot of lunch left, so Hunter and I caught up on old times. Hunter said that he and his wife, Susan, were doing great. There was just one major concern. Hunter's mother, Naomi, was not expected to live much longer, and she didn't know Jesus. When Hunter said that, I nearly dropped my fork. When Hunter and I were in college, neither of us were Christians. I was surprised and delighted to hear that he knew Jesus.

Hunter told me how he and Susan had tried repeatedly to tell his mother about Jesus, only to have her reject him, each time more decisively than the last. He said he and Susan had begun to pray that God would send someone else to talk with her. When he said that, something stirred inside me. I thought maybe God was prompting me to talk with her, so I asked where his mother was living. I thought maybe I could swing by and see her on my way to the airport, but Hunter informed me she was in the small town of Tahlequah, Oklahoma, 90 miles northeast of Tulsa. I immediately dismissed the thought, and soon I was back on a plane to Dallas.

In the days that followed, I couldn't get Naomi Malson off my mind. With a growing sense of urgency, it seemed God was still prompting me to talk with her. Two weeks later, I was sitting at my desk, and I whispered a prayer, "God, if you want me to talk with Naomi, get me to Tulsa, and I'll go the rest of the way." I didn't expect anything to come of it because I hadn't been to Tulsa in seven or eight years. Then, picking up a folder on our newest acquisition target, a number of large onshore gas fields, I asked one of my lead engineers to locate the largest company in the "play." I knew I would need to go see their president. Five minutes later, he called to tell me the company was head-quartered in Tulsa!

A couple of weeks later, I met with the president of that company in Tulsa, then I turned my rental car toward Tahlequah. I hadn't talked with Hunter since our lunch in Houston. That had been a month ago, and I wasn't sure if his mom was even still alive. I didn't even know where she lived other than "in a nursing home in Tahlequah." There was more I didn't know. The previous weekend, Hunter and Susan had visited his mom with one last effort to tell her about Jesus. She had utterly rejected Christ. Also in the previous week, two retired missionaries had gone to see her, and she had thrown them out, telling them, "Never set foot in my room again!" Had I known all that, I would have turned around. But I didn't, so I drove on.

I found Naomi in the hospital wing of the only nursing home in town. When I walked into her room, I could tell I startled her. I quickly introduced myself and told her that Hunter and I had been close friends in college. She smiled at that, and we shared small talk for a few minutes. Then she asked if I lived in Tahlequah. I told her I lived in Dallas. She was surprised, and asked why I was in Tahlequah. I said, "Mrs. Malson, I've come to Tahlequah to tell you how much Jesus loves you."

> *"Mrs. Malson, I've come to Tahlequah to tell you how much Jesus loves you."*

Almost instantly, tears started to roll down her cheeks. All she said was, "Oh my! Oh my!"

I asked her if I could tell her more about him. I read to her from John 14, where Jesus said he was going to prepare a place in heaven for all who trusted in him. After we had talked for thirty to forty minutes, I asked her if she would like to begin trusting Jesus and live the rest of her life for him. She said "yes" and quietly placed her faith in him. When the time came for me to leave, she squeezed my hand and said, "Thank you. This has been the best day of my life!"

I "floated" the ninety miles back to Tulsa and sat down for a late supper before going to the airport. I can't describe the feelings washing over me. Joy! Excitement! Peace! Contentment! I then drove on to the airport to catch my late night flight home. I boarded my plane and sank into my seat "dog tired." Sitting there, I felt God whisper, "You should see the party going on up here because of Naomi!" Instantly I thought of Jesus' statement that a party is thrown in heaven each time a drowning person is saved. I couldn't remember ever being so fully alive!

Naomi truly became a new person. Nurses and aides all wanted to know why she had become so cheerful and so kind. She asked Hunter and Susan to buy her a necklace with a cross, and she spoke openly about her new faith in Jesus. For six months in a nursing home bed, she was more fully alive than she had ever been in her life. Then in February in 1991, she stepped into heaven, into the arms of Jesus, the one who came to make her fully alive (John 10:10).

I'll ask you again. When are you most fully alive?

No matter what else we do with our lives, we won't experience life in all its fullness until we engage in the adventure of introducing spiritual seekers to Jesus Christ.

I'm most fully alive when I'm helping a spiritual seeker meet Jesus. I don't think I'm unusual in this. The book of Acts tells the dramatic stories of the most fully alive individuals who ever walked the planet. What were these individuals doing? Helping spiritual seekers meet Jesus. It's the final piece of the puzzle. No matter what else we do with our lives, we won't experience life in all its fullness until we engage in the adventure of introducing spiritual seekers to Jesus Christ.

THINK ABOUT IT...

1. Read some of the passages mentioned in this chapter that talk about Jesus' pursuit of "drowning" people. How would you describe his level of passion and commitment to reaching these people?

2. Read 2 Corinthians 5:18-20. Why do you think God gave us "the task of reconciling people to him"? (Why didn't he just do it himself?)

3. If you are a follower of Jesus, who were the people that helped you most when you were spiritually seeking? What did they do that was most helpful? What was not helpful?

4. If you are a spiritual seeker, is there someone who has been helpful as you consider the Christian faith? What have they done that is helpful? What has not been helpful?

5. Have you ever known the thrill of helping someone place his or her faith in Jesus? What were the circumstances? Looking back, how would you describe the experience?

6. How would you define "relational evangelism"?

7. Looking back at the four steps of relational evangelism described in this chapter, which of those steps are currently absent from you life? What would keep you from putting all four steps into practice?

EPILOGUE:
FOR THE LONG HAUL

*W*ell, there they are—nine simple pieces of the puzzle. None of them are complicated, and none of them are beyond your reach. But each one contributes a vital part to your experience of "life to the fullest." Just as true faith is more than intellectual assent to the truth, we have to go beyond merely *knowing* what the pieces are. We have to *live* them. Based on my experience, I want to offer a few suggestions.

Evaluate where you are today in each of these nine areas. Every year, members of our church take a confidential "Fully Alive Self-Assessment" that we developed a few years ago. It has proven to be invaluable as a monitoring tool for our relationship with Jesus. It highlights areas of our spiritual life that are going well, and it shines a light on areas that need improvement. I've included a copy of this survey for you in the appendix. I recommend that you make copies of the blank form so that you can take the survey from time to time. You can also download the survey from the church's website, www.friendswoodchurch.com.

The purpose of the survey isn't to stimulate bragging for doing well or condemnation for poor performance. The purpose is to help us take an honest look at key aspects of the most important relationship in our lives, our relationship with Jesus Christ.

It's helpful to focus on only one piece of the puzzle at a time. In fact, it's nearly impossible to make long-lasting, life-changing progress in several areas of our lives at the same time. Personally, I use the Self-Assessment to help me identify where my spiritual life needs attention. I then focus on a single area for a "season" that might last anywhere from one to twelve months. For instance, I spent several months this year focusing on my connection with God through prayer. During this time, I read passages of the Bible about prayer, learned from friends who have a vital life of prayer, and began practicing fresh ways to connect with the God of infinite love, power, and wisdom. When you choose one of the nine areas, you might find it helpful to go back and read that chapter in the book again.

The first four pieces of the puzzle—faith, prayer, Bible study, and worship—are primarily "vertical." They deal very specifically with our relationship with God. The last five pieces—community, holiness, money management, serving, and evangelism—are primarily "horizontal." They address our relationships with people. Of course, the "vertical" and the "horizontal" always overlap, but the "vertical" fuels the "horizontal." A vibrant, healthy relationship with God gives us the love, grace, strength, and wisdom we need to develop healthy relationships with others.

Finally, becoming fully alive in Jesus Christ is a process. It's a lifelong journey of getting to know someone who is infinite in love and power. For that reason, knowing God always inspires a sense of wonder. But we are human, so setbacks along the way are common. Make a commitment to grow spiritually in *this* season of your life. Now that you've read this book, you know how the puzzle fits together. You're ready for the most challenging and inspiring adventure life has to offer. You're ready to experience the fulfillment of the greatest promise on the planet! Remember this: Jesus Christ truly intends for you to experience "life to the fullest." He wants you to become fully alive. You can count on him, and you can count on his promise.

APPENDICES

FULLY ALIVE SELF-ASSESSMENT SURVEY

*G*od invites us to join him in a rich, rewarding relationship, but many pressures threaten to blur our focus and steal our hearts away from God. Jesus encouraged us to be careful so our growth is not "choked by life's worries, riches and pleasures." Instead, he wants us to have "a noble and good heart" so we can keep growing and be fruitful for him and his kingdom (see Luke 8:1-15).

This survey is designed to give people a spiritual checkup so they can determine areas where they are strong (so they can thank God for his grace and strength shown in their lives) and where they still need some work (so they can trust God and take steps toward improvement).

As you consider each of the nine pieces of the puzzle of being fully alive, be honest with God and with yourself. In the areas where you are doing well, take time to thank God. You may have several areas that need attention, but focus on only one, then take a few minutes to write a specific plan to make changes in that area. If you need help, talk to your small group leader, a wise friend, or a pastor.

Fully Alive Self-Assessment

Name (optional)_____

Date: _____

Rank how true these statements are about your life according to the following scale, where "1" is <u>Not True</u> and "10" is <u>Completely True</u>.

1. *Faith:* I am living my life, in every area and in every moment, under the absolute leadership of Jesus Christ.

   1___ 2___ 3___ 4___ 5___ 6___ 7___ 8___ 9___ 10___

2. *Prayer:* I have a close, vibrant conversational relationship with God that is nurtured and anchored by frequent time alone with Him.

   1___ 2___ 3___ 4___ 5___ 6___ 7___ 8___ 9___ 10___

3. *Bible Study:* My thoughts, feelings, and actions are consistently shaped by God's Word as I study it on a daily basis.

   1___ 2___ 3___ 4___ 5___ 6___ 7___ 8___ 9___ 10___

4. *Worship:* I have frequent times of worship, both with my church and in times alone, when I express passionate reverence, adoration, and devotion to God.

   1___ 2___ 3___ 4___ 5___ 6___ 7___ 8___ 9___ 10___

5. *Community:* I am part of a small group that is growing genuine Friendships, providing mutual Care, and building the Character of Christ in us.

1___ 2___ 3___ 4___ 5___ 6___ 7___ 8___ 9___ 10___

6. *Holiness:* I eagerly respond to God's instruction and correction in every area of my life as I passionately desire to please Him with all of my thoughts, words, and actions.

1___ 2___ 3___ 4___ 5___ 6___ 7___ 8___ 9___ 10___

7. *Money Management:* Knowing that all I have belongs to God, I follow Biblical guidelines for earning, spending, saving, borrowing, investing, and generous giving, which begins with my tithe.

1___ 2___ 3___ 4___ 5___ 6___ 7___ 8___ 9___ 10___

8. *Serving:* I am passionately serving where the Holy Spirit has directed me to serve.

1___ 2___ 3___ 4___ 5___ 6___ 7___ 8___ 9___ 10___

9. *Evangelism:* "With every sunrise" I am looking for "drowning people". I have a "Top 3" that I am building relationship with, that I pray for each day, and that I passionately seek to introduce to Jesus Christ.

1___ 2___ 3___ 4___ 5___ 6___ 7___ 8___ 9___ 10___

How to Lead a *Fully Alive* Group

This book is designed for individual study and small groups. The most powerful way to absorb and apply these principles is for each person to study and consider the application questions individually, then to discuss them in either a class or a group environment.

The questions and exercises at the end of each chapter are designed to promote reflection, application, and discussion. Order enough copies of the book for each person to have their own. For couples, encourage both to have their own book so they can record their individual thoughts and prayers.

A recommended schedule for a small group might be:

Week 1   Introduction to the material. The group leader can tell their own story, share their hopes for the group, and provide books for each person.

Weeks 2-10   Cover chapters 1-9, one chapter per week.

Week 11   Cover the conclusion of the book. Have the members of the group take the Fully Alive Self Assessment Survey and discuss their results and their plans for continued growth.

PERSONALIZE EACH LESSON

Make sure you personalize the principles and applications. At least once in each group meeting, add your own story, either a success or a failure, to illustrate a particular point.

Make the Scriptures come alive. For instance, if you are using a passage from the gospels, put your group in the scenes with Pharisees scowling, sinners rejoicing, and disciples often confused. Far too often, we read the Scriptures like it's a phone book, with little or no emotion. Paint a vivid picture for people. Provide insights about the context of the encounters with Jesus, and help people sense the emotions of specific people in each scene.

FOCUS ON APPLICATION

The book is written to help people become fully alive, so make sure you ask "So What?" questions each week in the group. Share how you are applying the principles in the chapter, and encourage them to take steps of growth, too.

THREE TYPES OF QUESTIONS

If you have led groups for a few years, you already understand the importance of using open questions to stimulate discussion. Three types of questions are *limiting, leading,* and *open.*

- *Limiting questions* focus on an obvious answer, such as, "What does Jesus call himself in John 10:11?" These don't stimulate reflection or discussion. If you want to use questions like this, follow them with thought-provoking open questions.

- *Leading questions* sometimes require the listener to guess what the person asking has in mind, such as, "Why did Jesus use the metaphor of a shepherd in John

10?" (He was probably alluding to a passage in Eze-kiel, but most people wouldn't know that.) The teacher who asks a leading question has a definite answer in mind. Instead of asking this question, he should teach the point and perhaps ask an open question about the point he has made.

- *Open questions* usually don't have right or wrong an-swers. They stimulate thinking, and they are far less threatening because the person answering doesn't risk ridicule for being wrong. These questions often begin with "Why do you think…?" or "What are some pos-sible reasons that…?" or "How would you have felt in that situation?"

Preparation

As you prepare to teach this material in a group, con-sider these steps:

1. Carefully and thoughtfully read the book. Make notes, highlight key sections, quotes, or stories, and com-plete the reflection sections at the end of each chapter. This will familiarize you with the entire scope of the content.

2. As you prepare for each lesson, read the corresponding chapter again and make any additional notes.

3. Tailor the amount of content to the time allotted. You may not have time to cover all the questions, so pick the ones that are most pertinent.

4. Add your own stories to personalize the message and add impact.

5. Before and during your preparation, ask God to give

you wisdom, clarity, and power. Trust Him to use your group to change people's lives.

6. Most people will get far more out of the group if they read the book each week. Order books before the class begins or after the first week.

ABOUT THE AUTHOR

Rick Baldwin grew up in South Texas. He attended Texas A&M University and graduated with a Bachelor of Science in Petroleum Engineering. After graduation, he worked for Sun Oil Company, later known as Oryx Energy Company, from 1976 to 1991. For five years with Sun Oil, he served as an engineer, and for the next ten years with the company, he worked in management. He was promoted to the position of Director of Acquisitions and charged with acquiring assets such as oil fields and oil companies. The largest purchase during that tenure was a $1.1 billion acquisition of North Sea, Indonesian, and South American assets from British Petroleum.

After a lengthy spiritual search, Rick became a Christian on October 10, 1984. Several years later, God led him to leave the oil business and become a pastor. He resigned from Oryx at the end of 1991 and entered Asbury

Theological Seminary in Wilmore, Kentucky. After graduating with a Masters of Divinity degree, he served as a pastor in the United Methodist denomination from 1995 to 1997.

At that time, Rick and Marie sensed God's leading to begin a non-denominational church in the Bay Area of Southeast Texas. With four other couples, they started meeting in a living room as Friendswood Community Church on January 4, 1998.

Rick's passion is introducing people to Jesus and helping them experience life to the fullest in Christ.

Rick and Marie have two sons, Justin and Daniel, who are following their father's footsteps at Texas A&M. Marie is a middle school math teacher. Rick enjoys track and field, and he's a huge fan of the Houston Astros!

About Friendswood Community Church

Friendswood Community Church

Come as you are

Shortly after Rick Baldwin's decision in 1984 to put his faith in Jesus Christ, he began to formulate the core values of his Christian life. Years later, they have been polished and honed, but the message remains unchanged:

1. Heaven and hell are real and eternity lasts forever.

2. God wants every single person to find forgiveness and eternal life through his Son, Jesus Christ.

3. The best and most fulfilling life possible is the life that is fully yielded to Jesus Christ.

4. The church is the hope of the world.

These concepts began to shape how Rick would think, act, and live. He didn't realize it at the time, but God was beginning a work in him that would result in the birth of Friendswood Community Church, which draws people from all around the Bay Area in Southeast Texas.

The concept that "the church is the hope of the world" was firmly engrained in Rick's mind. If Christians are to introduce their friends to Jesus Christ and help them become "fully alive," we need churches that are authentic and spiritually alive. On a winter day in late 1997, Rick, his wife Marie, and four other couples sensed God's leading to launch Friendswood Community Church to communicate these core values in a way that would change lives. Those same four core values still shape Friendswood Community Church today.

On Sunday, January 4, 1998, the first worship service took place in a living room. Following that service, the church began a six year odyssey holding worship services in various public schools. In 2002, God led the church to purchase 75 acres of land in the hope of reaching out to more people, and helping them realize Jesus' love for them. During the construction of the first building before the interior was finished out, the church held an unofficial worship service. To commemorate the fact that FCC exists to reach out to others, people wrote on the bare cement floor the names of three people they were praying would come to know Jesus Christ. Today, there are hundreds of names written beneath the carpet of the worship center, each written with the sense that Christ's heart beats for them. Some of those people whose names were written on the floor that day have already come to know Jesus.

On Christmas Eve, 2003, the first official worship service was held onsite. Since that time, attendance has increased to over 1600. On some Sundays, folding chairs are set up

in aisles and along walls to accommodate the growing crowd. To make sure people build strong, lasting relationships, people are encouraged to join small groups, called "Connections." Currently, about 500 people are involved in these groups.

One of the hallmarks of FCC is the spirit of service. It takes a great deal of work to "do church," but the 500 volunteers who make it happen at FCC think there's nothing else they could give their lives to

that would matter more.

Today, FCC continues to reach out in faith to others in the community, inviting everyone to "come as you are" to experience God's grace, love, power and guidance throughout daily life. FCC desires for everyone to embark on the greatest life adventure of knowing Jesus Christ through authentic community, a sense of mission and purpose, spiritual growth, and worship. We want every person to experience the incredible, full life that God intends for us all.

As Rick Baldwin says, "I know of no greater cause on planet Earth than the cause of Jesus Christ. Heaven and hell are real and eternity lasts forever, and God wants every person to find forgiveness and eternal life in his Son. The best and most fulfilling life is still the one that is fully yielded to Jesus Christ, and I know the church is still the hope of the world."

For more information,
go to www.friendswoodchurch.org

To Order More Copies of *Fully Alive*

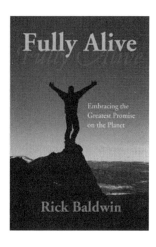

This book is designed to be used by individuals and groups. You can give copies to friends who want to understand more about what it means to be fully alive in Jesus Christ. Order copies for your staff at church or at work, for a class or a small group, or as gifts for your family and friends. People can use the discussion questions at the end of each chapter to stimulate interaction, gain insights, and make application of the principles in the book.

To order more copies
Go online to www.fccstore.com
Or call: 281-388-3533
Or write to:
Fully Alive
c/o FCC
2821 W. Parkwood
Friendswood, TX 77546

Payment options
Credit cards are accepted online. Checks are accepted by mail.